GREAT DAY HIKES
in
&
around *Napa Valley*

KEN STANTON

BORED FEET PRESS
MENDOCINO, CALIFORNIA
2008

© 1995, 2001, 2008 by Ken Stanton
Third edition, November 2007
Printed in the United States of America

Photographs by Ken Stanton, except photo on page 47 reprinted by
    permission of Society of California Pioneers
Illustration of rattlesnake grass (*Briza maxima*) by Elizabeth Petersen
Maps by Bob Lorentzen, Elizabeth Petersen, and USGS except maps
    on pages 66 and 179 by California Department of Parks and
    Recreation, and on page 143 by park staff, used by permission.
    Map on page 150 courtesy of Solano Land Trust, produced by
    Green Info Network, 2007.
Design by Elizabeth Petersen Graphic Design, Fort Bragg, CA
Production by Wendy Blakeway, Design Xperts
Edited by Nancy Kay Webb
Third edition edited by Donna Bettencourt

Published and Distributed by
Bored Feet Press
www.boredfeet.com
Post Office Box 1832
Mendocino, California 95460
707-964-6629 / 1-888-336-6199

Library of Congress Cataloging-in-Publication Data
Stanton, Ken
    Great day hikes in and around Napa Valley,
third edition/Ken Stanton.
        232 pp.
    Includes bibliographical references and index.
    ISBN 978-0-939431-35-9 : $16.00
    1. Hiking—California—Napa County—Guide-books. 2. Napa County
    (Calif.)—Description and travel—guide-books.   I. Title.

ISBN 978-0-939431-35-9

10 9 8 7 6 5

*Dedicated to all those who work selflessly
for open space in Napa County*

ACKNOWLEDGMENTS

In a book like this, many people play both large and small roles. I would like to thank them all including those I have inadvertently omitted. Thanks go first of all to Clyde Wise, Jo Maillard, Genji Schmeder and Ken Thatcher who know hiking trails in Napa intimately and pointed out many of the lesser known trails. My principal editor was Nancy Kay Webb, while John Hoffnagle, Joe Callizo and Bill Grummer also read and corrected the text. Thanks to publisher Bob Lorentzen and graphic artist Liz Petersen for making it easy to work together. Lucy Shaw and Reece Baswell provided the idea for this book. Mike Joell and Glen Mattila both gave their valuable time to hike Westwood Hills with me. Ellen Brannick and Mylon Pittman were essential sources for Skyline Park. Thanks to K.K. Burtis for her expertise on Native American history and Rod Broyles for trail updates at Bothe Park.

I was able to cover several days worth of work in a day thanks to Donna Howard and her wonderful staff at the Lake County Museum. Napa County Historical Society staff provided information for several chapters. Thanks to Jake Rugyt and Joe Callizo for native plant expertise. Also Jim Swanson and Teresa Le Blanc of California Department of Fish and Game for help on Cedar Roughs and Napa River Ecological Reserve. Greg Mangan and Scott Adams from BLM helped me find Blue Ridge Trail. Special thanks to Bob McKenzie for insights into life at Monticello and Berryessa Valley. Tom Klimowski and Roy Mason had a great part in the Rockville Hills chapter. Dean Enderlin generously allowed use of his *Trailside Geology of the Oat Hill Mine Road.*

In addition I'd like to thank Sandi Frey of Lakeport Library, Bob Carlson and Sherry Stone of Napa Parks and Recreation, Glenn Burch and Marla Hastings of State Parks, Napa River project manager Bob Sorsen, Ann and

continued on page 225

CONTENTS

WHAT KIND OF TRAIL
ARE YOU LOOKING FOR?

Trails Where Dogs Are Allowed (must be leashed all areas)

Cedar Roughs
Lake Hennessey
Alston Park
Napa River Trails
Rockville Hills Regional Park
Zem Zem Falls
Long Canyon
Hood Mountain Regional Park
Blue Ridge
Baldy Mountain
Cache Creek Wilderness

Trails with Handicapped Access

Petrified Forest
Napa River Trails

Trails Where Mountain Bikes Are Allowed

Mount St. Helena (fire road only)
Oat Hill Mine Trail
Bothe/Napa Valley State Park (designated trails only)
Alston Park
Napa River Trails
Skyline Wilderness Park
Rockville Hills Regional Park
Lynch Canyon-Newell Open Space

Sugarloaf Ridge State Park (designated trails only)
Hood Mountain Regional Park

Trails Where Horses Are Allowed

Oat Hill Mine Trail
Bothe /Napa Valley State Park (concessionaire too)
Alston Park
Skyline Wilderness Park
Lynch Canyon-Newell Open Space
Knoxville Wildlife Area
　　Zem Zem Falls
　　Long Canyon
Sugarloaf Ridge State Park including McCormick
Hood Mountain Regional Park
Blue Ridge
Baldy Mountain
Cache Creek Wilderness

Trails for Backpacking

Knoxville Wildlife Area
　　Zem Zem Falls
　　Long Canyon
Hood Mountain Regional Park (special permit)
Cache Creek Wilderness
　　Redbud Trail
　　Judge Davis Trail

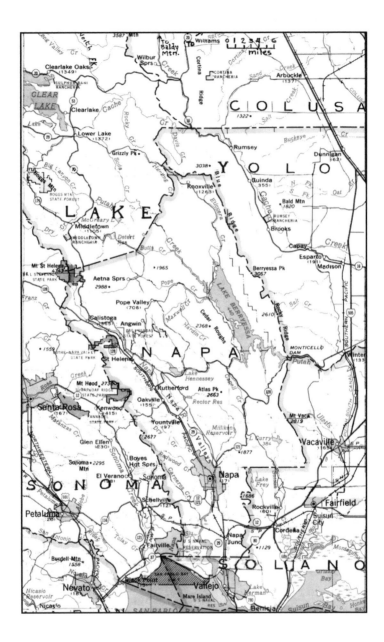

10

INTRODUCTION

Thirty years ago I was an idealist. Although an active hiker and climber, I owned no guide books nor wanted any. For me, a guidebook was an obstacle to the pure outdoor experience. Unfettered with someone else's thoughts, I could experience the wilderness on my own terms. Not that I wasn't prepared. All the necessities for a safe trip were stowed in the old Kelty, but the load was light. I took the minimalist approach, no camera, no flashlight, no tent and certainly no guidebook.

At last shelf count, my hiking, climbing and international travel guidebooks numbered 125. Times changed and so did I. When the National Park Service imposed quotas for heavily traveled areas of the Sierra Nevada in the 1970s, I balked. A High Sierra bureaucracy seemed an oxymoron. I wanted to go wherever and whenever it suited me. Today the wisdom of their decision is obvious. No place is an island, and resource management, including quotas, is imperative.

I still struggle, though, with the guidebook issue. "Won't a hiking guide increase traffic and diminish the solitude you seek?" people ask. Yes, but many actions we take are two-edged. John Muir struggled with the same issue. The father of the conservation movement would rather have spent his time outdoors than at his writing desk. Muir once wrote that after spending some time in the city, he returned to Yosemite and took the only serious fall of his career, knocking him unconscious. He reprimanded himself: "That is what you get by intercourse with stupid town stairs and dead pavements."

Yet he chose to write of Yosemite for a world audience, pleading for its preservation, knowing only wide spread public support could save it. No one doubts the wisdom of his decision, despite the four million visitors a year who threaten to love it to death. That is a problem for our generation to deal with.

Although most Napa natives prefer to keep their own trails to themselves, the reality is that for at least thirty-five years, visitors have accounted for half of outdoor recreation in Napa County. Unless population reaches stasis, that figure will increase. That is bad news for some locals, but it can be good news too. The more people know and love these hills, the stronger the efforts to save them from development.

One of the higher purposes of a guide is to inform and seek support for worthy causes such as the Oat Hill Mine Trail. The old freight wagon road near Calistoga, closed to vehicles since 1979, is so rich in historical, geological and botanical wonders that it wins my vote as the finest hiking trail in this guide. Landowner/developers posed a serious threat in 1990 when they illegally attempted to bulldoze and widen the road. This was the first step in their proposal to place a dozen multi-million dollar ranchettes on oak-studded hilltops overlooking Calistoga. The attempt was stopped but subsequently an alternate access was illegally cut. Ten years later, like a recurring nightmare, a real estate developer nearly bought this same parcel. Some fast action by the Land Trust of Napa County saved this key parcel by buying it outright for eventual transfer to state parks.

Other areas of concern are Napa's two state parks: Bothe-Napa Valley and Robert Louis Stevenson. The new millennium is signaling a brighter future for California state parks after a decade of dwindling financial support. Maintenance projects long deferred are receiving attention, and new personnel are relieving the burdens of overworked staff. Still, the need for volunteers remains constant. At Bothe Park, volunteers are always being sought to keep the visitor center open, maintain trails and buildings, and help with annual events like the Old Mill Days in October. At Robert Louis Stevenson State Park, the acceptance of a General Plan that would allow basic visitor services is long overdue and still nowhere in sight.

Why in the world has there been no hiking guide to Napa County until now? The answer seems obvious — Napa is wine country, not a hiking destination. Even as this guide was planned, the doubts remained. Could I find enough material to fill a book? Many of the hikes originally seen as likely candidates were eliminated, and usually for one reason — lack of full public access.

Napa County was once a quiet, drowsy backwoods, where prunes and walnuts were as common as the grape. Most of the hillsides were, even then, private property, but access was easier. You just let your neighbor know you were taking the mare for a ride, and closed the gate behind you. Starting in the mid 1960s, the success of wine led to a new population influx. Hillside vineyards replaced fir forests and chaparral slopes, and every wealthy San Franciscan wanted a chateau on forty acres overlooking Napa Valley. Beginning in the 1970s, property owners' growing fear of lawsuits led to fences, signs, and closures. Suddenly, land accessible for decades was off limits. There are probably few serious hikers today who can honestly say they've never done a bit of discreet trespassing, but this kind of thing cannot be advocated nor work as a solution.

It is a curious fact that in Napa, not a single county-owned-and-operated park exists. The county was way ahead of its time in 1968 when it established the revolutionary agricultural preserve, which has single-handedly prevented Napa from becoming another bedroom community of the Bay Area. Napans have since expressed further support for this concept by passing Measure J, extending the preserve to the year 2020.

Yet Napa County is equally far behind in supplying bona fide recreational access to its citizens. In 1974 a county-appointed committee was asked to address this issue. Their 150-page report, critical of the county, was as visionary in its concept and recommendations as was the agricultural preserve. This report, *Napa County's Park and Recreation Plan*, was never adopted due to lack of public support. Today nearly all of the plan's major components which have become reality have been implemented by other agencies.

Napa County's Park and Recreation Plan was submitted in March 1976 after two years of work, including consultation with local agencies and numerous public hearings. The committee was quick to point out that, "In contrast to almost all other California counties, Napa County at present time does not budget money on a regular basis for the creation, operation, and maintenance of Park or Recreation areas and facilities at the county level." They also made it clear that "the county has the basic responsibility among local governments for the preparation, adoption, and maintenance of a countywide parks and recreation plan."

The basic elements of the plan were:

1) Development of county parks on land in public ownership;
2) A system of county scenic roads;
3) A system of riding and hiking trails to connect with all county, state and federal recreation areas;
4) Bicycle routes using public road rights-of-way (Southern Pacific Railroad track line considered a desirable route separated from the roadway); and
5) Rest areas.

Highest on their list of priorities for county parks was Skyline County Park, followed by Valley Oak County Park (Napa River Ecological Reserve) and Lake Hennessey Recreation Area. Alternate suggestions included the 2,232-acre Milliken Reservoir area and the 5,200-acre Rector Reservoir area, both in public lands.

The most far-reaching and exciting idea in the plan was called the Napa Crest Trail. The committee envisioned a one hundred-mile loop trail for hikers and horseback riders, following the eastern and western ridge lines of Napa Valley from Napa to Mount St. Helena. Connector trails would hook up with all park and recreation areas, public and private. For example, a hiker could start at Bothe-Napa Valley State Park, connect with the Napa Crest Trail and finish at Sugarloaf Ridge State Park in Sonoma County. They also proposed cross-valley trails and designated one day loop trails.

What has happened in the thirty-one years since this remarkable proposal? Skyline Wilderness Park became a reality in 1980 with the county playing a minor role. At the public's urging, the state-owned land was leased to the county, which in turn leased it to Skyline Park Citizens Association, a private group operating the park today. Napa River Ecological Reserve was born when the state purchased the development-threatened property and turned it over to Fish and Game for management. Lake Hennessey is still owned by the City of Napa with limited boating and walking access. Proposed day-use camps and trails on the lake's east side were not developed. The Napa Crest Trail has been the biggest disappointment. Little else from the plan has been implemented. The county has long maintained it has no wish to be in the park management business. Although it endorses the concept of recreational access, the voting public has balked. In 1992 a ballot measure for an Open Space District was turned down by Napa County voters.

The city of Napa, on the other hand, has nearly forty regional, community and neighborhood parks. It also has begun a system of trails that will interconnect with two larger trails now in the development stage, the Bay Trail and the Bay Area Ridge Trail. The Bay Trail is a 400-mile multiuse path that will circle San Francisco and San Pablo Bays. Currently 60 percent finished with 240 miles of trail, it will connect nine Bay Area counties and forty-two shoreline cities. It dovetails with the city's Napa River Trail at John F. Kennedy Park.

Also passing through Napa is the Bay Area Ridge Trail, first conceived in the 1960s by the late visionary conservationist William Penn Mott. The Bay Area Ridge Trail Council is a grassroots organization that seeks to complete the 500-mile trail that would follow the mountains encircling the greater Bay Area. As of this writing, nearly 300 miles are dedicated. Five of those miles are found in Skyline Wilderness Park.

Another proposal, the Napa Valley Trail, would start at Cutting's Wharf, connecting with the Napa River Trail, and continuing along the length of the river to its source at Mount St. Helena. Due to intense rural and urban land use, implementing this trail would be difficult.

Earlier the question arose, would there be sufficient material to fill a Napa hiking guide? The answer of course is yes. Even after pursuing county trails for twenty-eight years, I was delighted to find many new to me. I'm confident most readers will discover hikes they weren't aware of before.

Great Day Hikes in and around Napa Valley helps readers find 200 miles of trails, 100 miles of those new since the first edition, about 60 of those new since the second edition. They range from casual walks suitable for small children to endurance contests fit for a Nepalese sherpa. Some of these hikes in state and city parks will be known by many locals. Others, on state- or federally-owned land or on easements through private land, you could drive past without knowing they exist. Most of the trails are in Napa County. For those feeling a need to "step out," I included hikes in adjoining counties — Sonoma, Lake, Yolo, and Solano.

The last ten years have seen a renaissance of new trails for Napa County. Skyline Park's Rim Rock Trail was completed, offering a far more satisfying loop trip. In the hills east of Yountville, the first segment of the Rector Ridge Trail is now open, with extension plans as far as famed Stag's

Leap. And in October 1999 the long awaited Palisades Trail opened. When combined with the Table Rock and Oat Hill trails, it provides one of the most unique hiking adventures in the greater Bay Area.

The Jack and Bernice Newell Open Space has opened but due to access issues, the only entrance at this time is from Lynch Canyon in Solano County. Situated in American Canyon and abutting Lynch Canyon Open Space, it has five miles of trail and fire road for hikers, equestrians and cyclists. Its 640 acres consist of mostly open rolling hills with tremendous views of the Delta, but include live oak forest and riparian corridor, rich wildlife country for nesting golden eagles and many other raptors. Early in the millennium, Skyline Park's River to Ridge Trail opened to serve as a connector between Kennedy Park and Skyline Park. Three miles of recently aligned and installed multiuse paved trail have already made the partially completed Napa River Trail a popular outing.

Over in the Lake District, or east county, an explosion of new opportunities has arisen. In 2005 the new 8,000-acre Knoxville Wildlife Area managed by California Department of Fish and Game opened to the public. Two hikes there are featured in this guide: Long Canyon and Zem Zem Falls, but many more trailheads and trails exist. Cedar Roughs became a federally designated wilderness area in 2006, and plans by the Bureau of Land Management to improve old trails and establish new trails are underfoot. The Pope Creek to Putah Creek Trail is partially open from the Putah Creek side, but easement issues have stalled its completion.

Something extraordinary happened in the Napa County elections of November 2006. The voters approved Measure I, an initiative to establish a Regional Parks and Open Space District, marking the beginning of a new era. Napa was the last county to adopt a park district in the Bay Area. According to the Napa County government website, "The District is authorized to plan, improve, and operate a system of public parks, trails, outdoor recreational facilities, and outdoor science and conservation education programs, as well as to protect and preserve natural areas, wildlife habitat and other open space resources." It means that 120,000 acres of public land, formerly inaccessible, will be available to all for walking, hiking, biking, fishing and picnicking, and that municipal watersheds will be better protected. A committee of five volunteer District directors will oversee operations. All residents of the county and anyone who visits will benefit from this giant step forward.

In 2007 another historic decision came down. After twenty-seven years the county board of supervisors voted to reactivate easement rights on the Oat Hill Mine Trail, a road that had been abandoned in 1979. By a 3-2 vote the supervisors forged a management agreement with the newly formed Napa Regional Parks and Open Space District to "repair, restore and operate the Oat Hill Mine Road and the westernmost .27 mile of Aetna Springs Road as a non-motorized recreational trail." This was long awaited and exciting news for many hikers and outdoor enthusiasts who had dreamed of this for thirty years.

The decision has several positive effects. The 1) It will actually reduce liability for adjacent landowners, putting the responsibility on the county. 2) It will mean restoration of a unique and historic recreational asset that some feel should be on the National Register of Historic Places. 3) It will reduce erosion and pollution and improve water quality in the affected watersheds. For hikers, bikers and equestrians, it opens a one-way through hike of eight miles from Calistoga to the Aetna Springs Road, perhaps one of the finest trails in all the coastal ranges of California. For hikers, a one-way car-shuttled hike can now be done along the Palisades Trail to Aetna. As stated earlier, a true renaissance era of hiking trails is here.

Napa Valley lies in a climatic transition zone between the cool moist air of the coast and the warm dry air of the Central Valley. The Mayacmas Mountains on the west are wetter and more wooded, suitable for hiking in summer and fall. On the east the Vaca Mountains are drier and exposed to the sun, making them a good winter and spring destination. The best seasons to hike in Napa County are spring and fall, with many fine days between storms in winter. Summer is often too warm.

WINTER is a great season to hike if you are properly prepared, with extra clothes and rain gear in your pack. The trails are quiet, the air clear, and views from ridgetops outstanding. On cold days, with wind chill near freezing, a thermos of hot beverage is great for the spirits. If it's a decision between the steaming liquid and my big telephoto lens, I bring the thermos every time. When the dreaded tule fogs slink in for an extended stay, and the valley is dank and miserable, the ridgetops can bath in glorious sunshine. Recommended hikes: Oat Hill Mine Trail — both west and east sides — Rim Rock Trail in Skyline Park, Mount St. Helena, Lake Hennessey.

SPRING is the most pleasant and rewarding season. Temperatures are moderate, the hills are green, and rains have brought wildflowers. On many warm days short pants and short sleeve shirts can be worn, but keep extra clothes in the pack for sudden weather changes. In stable weather, fogs will push in from the coast and cover the valley until late morning. You'll be in the sun in the hills above 1,000 feet or so. Recommended hikes: Oat Hill Mine Trail, Skyline Trail, Blue Ridge, Rockville Hills, Sugarloaf Park, Westwood Hills, Mount St. Helena, Baldy Mountain.

SUMMER can be the least desirable time in Napa. The air is hazy, temperatures high, grasses and watercourses have turned dry. Nevertheless, there are good options. Try early morning and evening, or even moonlight hiking. Choose the shady creek trails on the valley's west side or Skyline Park. Bring water, a hat, sunscreen and forget the rain gear. Watch for the appearance of fog, it means cooler temperatures for a few days. Recommended hikes: Redwood and Ritchey Canyon Trails in Bothe Park, Marie Creek Trail in Skyline, Napa River Trails.

FALL is a beautiful time in the valley. The weather is often stable, morning air is crisp, and deciduous trees and vines turn color. The yellows, reds, and pinks of black oak, sycamore, and dogwood leaves make a brilliant contrast to the dominant evergreen forest. Shorts and T-shirts are appropriate wear as late as Halloween. Recommended hikes: Petrified Forest, Buckeye and Lake Marie Trails at Skyline, Coyote Peak at Bothe, Stebbins Cold Canyon Reserve.

Note: Weather extremes can be severe at Baldy Mountain, Cache Creek, Blue Ridge and Mount St. Helena.

Explorers at cave along Oat Hill Mine Trail, East Side

MOUNT SAINT HELENA

Robert Louis Stevenson State Park is Napa's largest

DIRECTIONS: From Calistoga, drive north on Highway 29 almost 8 miles until signs indicate you have arrived at Robert Louis Stevenson State Park. There are parking lots on either side of the road. The trail begins on the west side.

DISTANCE: 5 miles one way

GRADE: Strenuous

ELEVATION GAIN: 2,100 feet

BEST TIME: Spring, fall. Once or twice a winter snows provide fun for snowshoers, skiers, and kamikaze mountain bikers.

INFO: Bothe-Napa Valley State Park, 707/942-4575

FACILITIES: Several picnic tables. Find water 2 miles north on Highway 29 at Rattlesnake Spring.

Kana'mota was the Wappo Indian name for Mount St. Helena, meaning human mountain. For thousands of years, Kana'mota was the geographical and spiritual heart of Wappo land. The Wappo tell the story of Coyote and his grandson Chicken Hawk, who, with his two sisters, flies to the dry top of Kana'mota when it rains for twenty days and nights. All others are drowned by the flood waters. When the waters recede, Coyote rebuilds each house, places a feather there for each person, and brings gifts of speech, movement, laughter, and food from the Moon so they may live again.

21

The mountain remains today a spiritual center and place of prayer for the Wappo people.

The Mexican period in northern California was short but influential. The Franciscans founded the last of the missions in Sonoma in 1823. As the story goes, when Father Jose Altimira saw the great mountain to the north, its summit in profile reminded him of a saint's tomb he had seen in an abbey in Rheims, France. He named it for Helena, mother of Constantine the Great.

The Mexican government was fearful of the Russian colony at Fort Ross. In an effort to prevent Russian expan-sion, they began in the 1830s to grant land to trusted individuals. These Mexican land grants were given to Mexican citizens or Americans who changed citizenship. In 1839 Dr. Edward Bale was given *Rancho Carne Humana*, one of the largest land grants in Napa County, stretching from mid-valley to the foot of Mount St. Helena. At the southern and western base of Mount St. Helena was Rancho Mallacomas (*Moristul y Plan de Agua Caliente*), given to Jose Berryessa in 1843.

The Mexican expansion played only a small part in the Russians' decision to leave. Crop failure and depletion of the sea otters had made Fort Ross an economic failure. Before they left in 1841, scientist Il'ia Voznesenski made a final expedition into the interior to conduct botanical and ethnographic studies. With his companion Chernykh they made the first recorded ascent of the tallest peak in the region, leaving a copper plaque affixed to a rock at the summit. Like Father Altimira, they also christened the peak Mount Saint Helena. Back home in Saint Petersburg, Voznesenski would spend the rest of his life cataloguing his remarkable collection.

The same year the Mexican government bid farewell to the Russians, the Bidwell-Bartleson Party crested the Sierra Nevada. A whole new problem had arrived. Overland par-ties of American settlers slowly settled the Napa Valley in the 1840s. Following the Bear Flag Revolt, California became part of the United States in 1846. The Mexican land grants,

Mount St. Helena viewed from the Oat Hill Mine Trail

if not tied up in court over property disputes, were parceled and sold to the newcomers. After the gold rush of 1849, Napa Valley quickly filled with Americans.

In 1850 the Bull Trail was carved out of the woods by volunteer effort. It followed an Indian trail from Calistoga to Middletown. This steep, narrow grade was the official road for eighteen years. Cattle and hogs, sometimes hauling sleds, were driven to market from Lake County, but it was too rugged for wheeled vehicles.

Miners meanwhile kept the gold fever alive by prospecting in the hills. They finally found their own El Dorado in the form of cinnabar over near Pope Valley in 1861. Cinnabar's by-product, quicksilver, was in heavy demand for gold refining in Nevada. Shipments increased through the 1860s until entrepreneur John Lawley saw his cue. Knowing the railroad was coming to Calistoga, he built a new road over the mountain to connect the mines with the railhead. Lawley's Toll Road was finished in 1868, designed and maintained with the mines' freight wagon traffic in mind. He and his family would collect toll at the top of the grade for more than half a century.

The last quarter of the nineteenth century was the golden age for Napa County's mining industry. Mines like the Redington in Knoxville, the Aetna and Oat Hill near Pope Valley, and the Mirabel and Great Western on Mount St. Helena made this area the second richest quicksilver strike in United States history. Gold and silver were also found at the Silverado Mine on Mount St. Helena and at the Palisades Mine near Calistoga.

A spinoff industry developed as a result of mining's success: road agentry. Stagecoaches loaded with payroll for the mines were often robbed by highwaymen on the Lawley Road. Quite often they were amateurs who needed some extra cash. Commonly they were friends or acquaintances. As historian Anne Roller Issler has said, "Like deer on the mountain, stage robbers were neighbors until they became game."

Others, like Lake County resident Buck English, made a career of stage robbing. Buck was in and out of jail most of his adult life for cattle rustling, stagecoach heists and various other crimes. In 1895 his last robbery took place on Lawley's Toll Road near the Mountain Mill House and led to the most exciting manhunt in Napa County history. He escaped with $1,000 and disappeared for three days, wearing out his shoes traveling the rugged Oat Hill country. He was finally apprehended on the Mount George Grade near Napa after a wild shootout. San Quentin's prisoner number 16426 spent most of his remaining years behind bars.

The greatest period of gold and silver mining came to an end around the turn of the century. After 1900, quicksilver mines began a slow decline. Horse-drawn wagons now had to share the road (unwillingly) with the automobile. As the highwayman disappeared, stagecoaches stopped carrying firearms by 1910. By 1915 horse-drawn stages were replaced by auto buses. Around this time, Mount St. Helena's other toll road, the Ida Clayton, went public. Increasing public pressure and falling revenues forced Mollie Patten, John Lawley's daughter, to sell the Lawley Toll Road to the state. By 1924 the new highway left Mollie and the

Toll House by the wayside. An era had passed.

The last major road on the mountain was built in 1935. E.A. Erickson was state forest ranger based at Las Posadas Forest in Angwin. He successfully lobbied Sacramento for a lookout tower on Mount St. Helena and for a fire road to the summit. Just as the Civilian Conservation Corps was finishing the fire road, they were called away suddenly without expecting to return. Ignoring the carefully placed survey markers, the last quarter mile was bulldozed in a hurry, straight uphill.

Public access lands and resorts have been on the rise from the 1930s to the present. The trend started with trout farms like Smith's off the Ida Clayton Road and Russel's in Troutdale Canyon. Later the old Silverado mining town site became a dude ranch offering horseback rides to the summit. Girl Scouts ran a camp near the Mountain Mill House. The most significant change came in 1949 when Norman Livermore gave the first forty acres of land for budding Robert Louis Stevenson Memorial Park. It has enlarged over the years to 5,273 acres. California State Parks improved the trail to the monument and connected it with the fire road, now the main route to the summit.

For well over a hundred years a trail of one sort or another has cleaved the brush and skirted the volcanic outcrops to the top. C.A. Menefee's history of Napa, Lake, Sonoma and Mendocino counties in 1873 states that "a good trail has been made for the accommodation of tourists which renders the ascent easy." Whether ten miles of trail are ever easy depends on your condition, but another of his statements gives one pause: "Towards the north, Clear Lake lies mapped out in plain view." Today only summits surrounding the lake, like Mount Konocti, are visible. Whether Menefee made the ascent or not, it's clear that Mount St. Helena has one of the oldest recreational trails in the county.

Table Rock, a part of the spectacular Palisades, was included in the state park in 1993. Four years later, local environmentalists concluded a thirty-two-year quest when all the Palisades east to Oat Hill Mine Trail became part of Robert Louis Stevenson State Park. The trail officially opened in autumn 1999 and is now generally conceded to be the finest hiking trail in Napa County.

TRAIL NOTES:

From the west parking lot, wooden steps lead to a large pleasant clearing. Lawley's Toll House stood against the hillside; some of its foundation is still there. The stage-coaches would pass right in front, after they paid toll and Mollie Patten lifted the gate. A remnant of the original road can be traced from the clearing's north end to the present highway. Picnic tables are scattered around the site of an old croquet ground, also used as a bocce ball court before World War II.

At the trail sign, the path immediately leads into a mixed evergreen forest of madrone, black oak, Douglas fir, tan oak and bay. Easy switchbacks lead up the steep hill for more than ½ mile. Then the forest thins as manzanita and knobcone pine appear. At the last switchback stop for a view of the Palisades to the southeast, then descend to the granite marker commemorating Robert Louis Stevenson's honeymoon visit in the summer of 1880. At that time the clearing was open enough for a view of Napa Valley. All the Douglas fir on the mine tailings flat beside the monument are probably post mine-closure age, that is, 1877 or later. Stevenson took notes that summer for *The Silverado Squatters*, one of his minor works but still the best book written about Napa Valley.

The upper shaft of the Silverado Mine is uphill to the left. This is an intriguing place to explore but be aware — a significant amount of rock has fallen here in recent years. One climber dislodged a one ton boulder from the seventy-five-foot north face in 1993. Missing his rope by inches, it split in two on impact and careened downhill to the monu-ment flat. Fortunately no one was hurt.

The roughest part of the 5-mile trail leads past the monu-

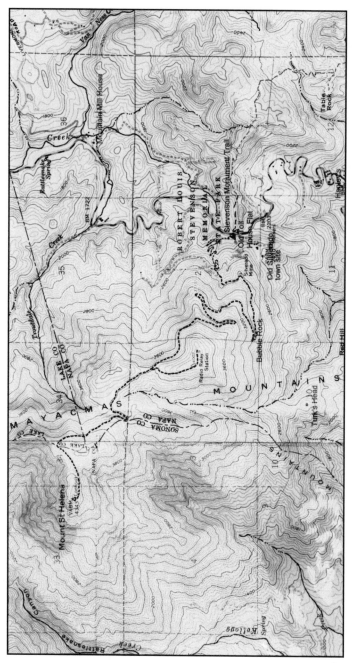

27

ment to the fire road at ⅞ mile. Along this segment you leave the seclusion of shady fir forest and enter the bright, sunlit world of chaparral and stubby knobcone pine. At mile 1 you are directly above the upper mine shaft and looking straight down the Napa Valley. If it's not smoggy, foggy or hazy, you'll see the twin-summited peak of Mount Diablo sixty-six miles south. The fire-tested south-facing slopes stretching before you support eight species of manzanita, plus chamise, ceanothus, toyon, coffeeberry and mountain mahogany. The best spring flower displays are seen along here: bush poppies, chaparral pea, Indian warrior and monkeyflower.

At 1¼ miles you pass a gathering of gray pine, bay, and canyon live oak that somehow escaped the last century of fires. Beyond is the Bubble Rock. Hikers get a kick out of watching climbers scale the vertical and overhanging pocket ladders. In this area are many more fantastically shaped pillars of old lava and ash flow of varying degrees of reliability. The most solid of these crags are now considered some of the best rock climbing in the Bay Area.

The road ahead will turn rocky in places but generally reflects the wishes of the road builders who wanted an easy grade to carry materials for the summit lookout tower. As you climb you'll see Blue Ridge to the east, the prominent backbone of the Vaca Mountains that separates the North Coast Ranges from the Central Valley. The Sierra will also be visible on a clear day.

At a big switchback at 2¼ miles, look for 7,056-foot Snow Mountain in the southern portion of Mendocino National Forest. The massive bulk of Mount St. Helena's south peak shades your trail until a trail junction at 3¼ miles. Here a partially paved trail, slightly shorter than ½ mile, leads to the 4,003 foot top of the south peak. In 1987 Telecommunications Incorporated built an observation deck with a display showing air line miles to various regional peaks. The topmost forty acres is an inholding of the Bureau of Land Management, which leases the land to companies owning communications equipment. This is a satisfying destination for many hikers. Views are excellent to the south, east and west.

Cross the flat, so-called summit plateau once erroneously described in the 1873 *Bancroft's Tourist Guide to Napa Valley* as the crater of the extinct volcano. Almost imperceptibly you pass over the headwaters of Kimball Creek at 3¾ miles. It leads to the city of Calistoga's municipal water supply at the foot of Kimball Canyon. Start to climb again at mile 4. Look for giant chinquapin and sniff for the sickly sweet smell of tobacco brush. The waters of Lake Berryessa are now visible below Berryessa Peak.

At 4½ miles a junction leads to one of the middle peaks. The 100-foot microwave tower recently installed leaves one aghast. Soon you arrive at Windy Point and the first view of the Geysers' white plumes. The few sugar pines around provide welcome sun relief. The last ¼ mile is steep. You will pass the rare Rincon Ridge buckbrush, a mound-forming ceanothus up to eighteen inches high, found only on this mountain and near Santa Rosa. Your climb

Fiddleheads announce the arrival of spring

ends after 5 miles at the 4,339-foot summit (the official height was lowered four feet by USGS researchers in 1994). Both the middle and north peaks are part of a 200-acre inholding of the Livermore family. The fire lookout tower, which had been unmanned for several years due to budget cuts, was dismantled in January 1996. Next to where the tower once stood is an exact replica of the Russian plaque marking the first ascent in 1841. Words are written in English and Russian for you bilingual hikers.

The summit slopes gently west to what the state mineralogist tagged the Giant's Causeway in 1885. This is the top of columnar andesite cliffs that buttress the north peak. Notice the five-sided jointing similar to Devil's Postpile in the eastern Sierra. The steep north slopes drop into remote Rattlesnake and Bradford canyons where black bear, bobcat, fox and mountain lion roam. From here views can be breath-

taking of the Pacific Ocean, San Francisco and Sierra summits. You might also see California's share of the Cascade Range, Mount Lassen and Mount Shasta, the latter 192 miles distant.

Climbing a rock outcrop on the mountain

PALISADES TRAIL VIA TABLE ROCK TRAIL

Napa County's best hike

DIRECTIONS: To reach the Palisades Trail, you must hike down the Table Rock Trail to its end or ascend the Oat Hill Mine Trail to its summit. The best one-way hike will take in all three trails, north to south, starting at Robert Louis Stevenson State Park. Most people leave a shuttle car at the junction of Highway 29 and Silverado Trail (Oat Hill Mine trailhead), and then drive to the Table Rock trailhead. Drive Highway 29 north from Calistoga to the summit, where Table Rock Trail begins at the east parking lot across the highway from the Mount St. Helena trailhead.

DISTANCE: The combination of the Table Rock, Palisades, and Oat Hill Mine trails is 10⅞ miles. From Table Rock trailhead, it's 2⅛ miles to Table Rock (start of Palisades Trail), 6 miles to the Holm's place where you meet the Oat Hill Mine Trail.

GRADE: Strenuous

BEST TIME: Spring, autumn

WARNINGS: The Palisades Trail is narrow and steep-sided and was designed expressly for foot travel only. No bikes or horses are allowed. If you approach the Palisades Trail via the Oat Hill Mine Trail, you must negotiate nearly 2,000 feet of elevation gain before reaching the Palisades Trail junction.

Made possible by a State Parks purchase in 1997, the Palisades Trail finally opened in October 1999 amid celebratory hikes, parties, and fanfare that included articles in such prominent magazines as Sunset *and* Outside. *Creation of this long awaited and eagerly anticipated trail was a tour de force for local conservationists who first conceived the idea thirty five years ago, then lobbied ceaselessly until it became reality. Some of the prominent people behind it were Harry Tranmer, Ranger Bill Grummer, John Hoffnagle, the Livermore family and Joe Callizo.*

This five-star route has most everything: close-up views of volcanic cliffs, panoramic views of the Napa Valley, shady evergreen forests, flower-spangled meadows, mysterious grottoes fed by year-round seeping water, nesting peregrine falcons, and, in winter, a chance to see 100-foot-high ephemeral waterfalls. Combine this exquisite new 3⅞-mile trail with the spectacular Table Rock Trail and the dramatic Oat Hill Mine Trail for a 10⅞-mile extravaganza that is not to be missed.

TRAIL NOTES:

Ascend switchbacks through a cool forest of tan oak, big leaf maple, bay laurel and Douglas fir for several hundred feet until turning left onto a road. At ¼ mile Snow Mountain appears to the north on clear days. Resume climbing at a notch around ½ mile, leaving the highway behind.

Take the signed right fork at ⅝ mile and the road soon turns to trail again. Around mile 1 you pass the former park boundary prior to the Table Rock purchase of 1993. Great views of Bear and Cub valleys appear. The trail turns sharply right, then before a prominent rock outcrop it dives down and to the left. Use caution on this steep, loose section until your trail levels at a flat filled with wildflowers in spring.

Let the curving row of rocks lead you to an opening in the brush at 1¼ miles. Soon a second, steeper and looser descent follows. Be especially careful here — in recent years two hikers have sustained injuries necessitating evacuation by helicopter. Continue descending through grasses until you reach a pretty spot on tiny Garnett Creek at 1¾ miles. Cross the stream and start climbing again through mixed evergreen forest. Soon you come out among fantastic volcanic formations. On the distant ridgeline stands the distinctive T-Rex Rock, its dinosaur likeness best seen from here. The scene here is quite picturesque, especially when the little stream is running.

At 2 miles turn to the right (west) and scramble uphill toward a tableland of volcanics. **Exercise extreme caution** as you approach the edge of Table Rock at 2⅛ miles, which drops off sheer for 200 feet. Return the same way, or continue on the Palisades Trail.

At Table Rock the new trail sign says "Lasky Point 0.8 mile, Oat Hill Mine Trail 3.9 miles." The junction of the old and new trails was obvious when the Palisades Trail first opened, cut wide in anticipation of the characteristically speedy regrowth of chaparral. Slopes of buckbrush and chamise flank the stony trail as you head southeast. Behind you Mount St. Helena comes into view.

Ascend the first of many carefully placed rock steps, then at 2¼ miles as you stand directly under T-Rex Rock, you have a panoramic view of Napa Valley and at least four other counties. The summits of Mount St. John (2,375 feet)and Mount Veeder (2,677 feet) rise south of here on the crest of the Mayacmas Mountains which form the western rim of Napa Valley. In the next ¼ mile, you switchback steeply downhill with hand placed rock steps on the steepest sections. This portion was the most difficult to locate and build to park safety standards.

Before 2½ miles take note of a rocky, narrow section where trail crews used betonamit to break apart rock. Betonamit is a viscous expansion agent pored into drilled holes and allowed to work overnight like a quick form of frost heaving. You pass through an open forest of Douglas fir, madrone and bay trees, then, at the bottom of the descent, black oak. Traversing the hillside now, the path winds artfully under tree limbs and over steps made in rocky outcrops, making it a natural part of the landscape. Before 2⅝ miles, views of Garnett Canyon open up, the first of many into that watershed that accompany you all the way to Oat Hill Mine Trail.

Beyond 2⅝ miles a state park boundary sign indicates you've passed into the Lasky easement which continues for about ¼ mile. Please stay on the path so as not to jeopardize future access. Dramatic views of the Palisades cliffs appear at Lasky Point beyond 2⅞ miles. Watch carefully the next few steps over rock ledges. If you are lucky to be here when the maples turn color in fall, the contrast of bright yellow leaves with the brown and black volcanic rock is dramatic. Begin a gradual ascent as you pass back onto park property. Soon your trail crosses the first of nearly a dozen stream beds, the fords of which should not be a problem except after a prolonged rainstorm.

One of these crossings around mile 3 holds spice bush, indicating the proximate presence of water. In the fall seeds and husks of buckeye trees litter the trail. Begin a gradual descent around 3⅛ miles with the cliff close at hand. You make several more creek crossings that will be only rivulets or dry most of the year, then pass through a pleasant bay and maple forest before 3½ miles. Reach a long upland meadow at mile 4 that makes a fine lunch site on a cool day.

At 4⅜ miles a steep hillside pressed closely by cliffs on three sides holds a buckeye forest. In the autumn with the trees bare, save for the huge seeds on branch ends, it may look at first glance like an old fruit tree planting. After a grove of blue oaks, pass into a clearing at 4⅝ miles to find a trail sign and a private road junction. For the next ½ mile the trail is mostly uphill across an open grassy hillside. After crossing the next ridge, look for a massive dark colored cliff face about 150 feet high. Here is the historic, perhaps prehistoric, nesting cliff of the peregrine falcon. Their eyries

34

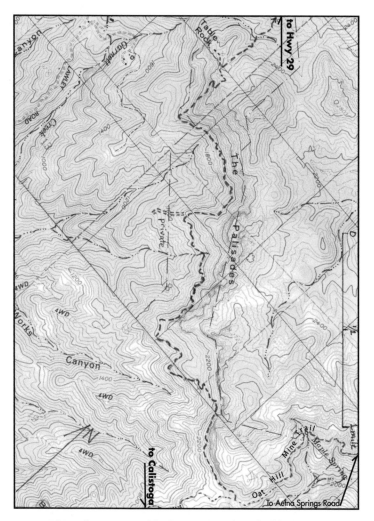

are on the white stained ledges more than half way up. This endangered raptor is the fastest animal in the world, clocked at diving speeds of 200 miles per hour.

In the wet months of the year a tiny but exquisite waterfall is seen right off the trail at 4⅞ miles. A mat of moss is backdrop for a curtain of water falling in a dozen individual streams. Soon you'll pass weirdly shaped pillars of volcanic

The dramatic Palisades from up close

stone, rock gargoyles, with a sturdy little fern called Sierra cliff brake (Pellaea brachyptera) growing under rocks scattered about this south facing hillside. Begin the last uphill climb on the trail.

Beyond 5⅛ miles, traverse beneath the cliffs themselves where a series of wet spots, springs, seeps and grottoes support spice bush, sword fern and other moisture loving plants. Another ¼ mile brings you close enough to lean against the base of cliffs one hundred feet high. Here you'll find a four-foot-wide, 80-foot-high chute formed by rainwater in the soft rock. From here you look down on the Oat Hill Mine Trail. At 5¾ miles a plaque in the cliff base commemorates the conservation efforts of the Nature Conservancy and the Napa County Land Trust. Dive into a shady oak and laurel forest, take two big switchbacks and come out at the historic Holm's place at mile 6 where two foundations and an apple orchard survive, leaving testimony to the homesteading Scandinavian family detailed in the next chapter. From here, turn right and go 4⅞ miles downhill to the Oat Hill Mine trailhead, or you can retrace your steps to your starting point, a longer but less steep hike.

OAT HILL MINE TRAIL, WEST SIDE

Old freight wagon road leads into the past

DIRECTIONS: Follow Highway 29 or Silverado Trail north until the two roads meet, .5 mile north of Calistoga. Park alongside either road or Lake Street, but avoid the small dirt lot at the trailhead. The trail begins at the metal gate.

DISTANCE: 4⅞ miles one way

GRADE: Strenuous

ELEVATION GAIN: 1,900 feet

BEST TIME: Spring

WARNINGS: The entire trail is now officially a county easement, but private property holdings are found at the start and near the end. Please stay on the trail unless you know exactly where those boundaries are.

The Oat Hill Mine Road might never have become an important thoroughfare of Napa County without the Pope Valley mining boom of the late 1800s. There are too many other stream valleys and low mountain passes to follow without the rocky and precipitous contours of the Palisades to deal with. Even with the heavy demand for the road, it took three separate attempts over twenty years to finally complete.

Site of Flynn Homestead

In 1861 John Newman was on a hunting trip near Aetna Springs when out of curiosity he picked up a rock. It was cinnabar (from which mercury or quicksilver is made), and by the next year he and John Lawley would form the Phoenix Mining Company, the first in Napa County. Others would follow — the Washington, Corona, Twin Peaks, Red Hill, and Silver Bow.

The railhead was brought to Calistoga by Sam Brannan in 1868, the same year John Lawley built his toll road over Mount St. Helena. Freight wagons carrying ore from these mines made the laborious trip to Butts Canyon Road into Middletown and over the toll road to Calistoga. Mining companies paid heavy fees for the privilege of using Lawley's road.

In 1872 cinnabar was found at the base of Oat Hill. It would be years before the mine was ready for production. However, over by Knoxville at the northeast end of Napa County, the Redington Mine was the county's biggest producer. The owners petitioned the county for a road from Calistoga, over the Palisades, past the Phoenix Mine to the Redington. Construction was begun in 1873 but halted before all was finished.

38

Today we can only speculate about the reasons for the halt. Funds may have run short, or perhaps enough of the road was completed to serve the company's needs. Lack of demand may also have been a factor. By 1876 when a second attempt was made to finish it, the price per flask of quicksilver had dropped from more than a hundred dollars to forty-four dollars, primarily due to overproduction.

Then in 1880 John Lawley built another road from the Pope Valley mines to join Lawley's Toll Road at the Mountain Mill House. Today called the Livermore Road, it saved teamsters fourteen grueling miles. That same year the Oat Hill Mine, producing by 1876, had outpaced the Redington. The Oat Hill was on its way to becoming the sixth largest quicksilver mine in the world. At first owned by local men, it was bought by an outfit in Boston and became the Napa Consolidated Company in the late 1870s.

As annual production rose at Napa Consolidated Mine, more profits were eaten up by toll road fees. Demand grew for a free and direct route to Calistoga. Napa Consolidated won the bidding to build the Calistoga-Oat Hill road for the county in 1892. Supervisor Newcomb then subcontracted the job to J.L. Priest of Chiles Valley. The rocky pass over the Palisades required blasting with dynamite, but apparently even the death of Priest did not delay completion of this segment that had stymied builders for twenty years. His brothers, William and Daniel Priest, finished the job by the contract date of June 1, 1893.

Even before completion, there were settlers on both sides of the Oat Hill Road. Irishman Patrick Flynn applied for and patented three homesteads on the Calistoga side, all within two miles of town. Just above the third and highest site, Flynn had a mining claim called the Leopard. He enjoyed the slow pace of traffic on the uncompleted Oat Hill, so in 1893 he was disgruntled when all the freight wagons began rumbling by. Flynn put up a gate with a lock, which the sheriff was obliged to cut. At the report of a second lock on the gate, the sheriff was not so amused. A stiff warning for

Flynn's arrest kept the road open after that. After Flynn died, his daughter Mamie lived on their land into the 1930s.

With the completion of the Oat Hill Mine Road, a retired Finnish ship carpenter named Karl Holm was able to homestead 160 acres at the high point of the road. In 1898, in a beautiful grove of trees under the ramparts of the Palisades, he built a stone house, a barn and planted an orchard inside a stone wall. Springs from under the Palisades provided water. By the next year his neighbor John Holm (probably his brother) also owned 160 acres. John Holm died in February 1902; his widow, Kristina, married Karl later the same year.

John's children lost their homestead in 1906 for nonpayment of property taxes totalling less than five dollars. Karl and Kristina lost their place in 1910 for delinquent property taxes and a small loan default. According to Anthony Cerar, who lived at the Oat Hill Mine in those days, a German named Sperling lived at the site until his death in 1919.

The Oat Hill Mine was worked continuously until 1909 employing sixty whites and 120 Chinese. A town built up around it with families living in houses that covered the nearby hillsides. Oat Hill had its own general store, drug store, sawmill, slaughter house, blacksmith shop, post office, two boarding houses and a public school. It was here that Anthony Cerar went for three years of his education. He says the Calistoga road, as it was known to people on the Oat Hill side, was the only way to town until 1924. People of average means couldn't afford the Lawley Toll Road until it went public. He remembers watering troughs for freight wagon horses located at Flynn's, Holm's, Maple Springs, Corona Mine and the Oat Hill Mine. Cerar likes to tell anyone who listens that contemporary names for the Holm's place like China Camp and the Halfway House are false — "modern Hollywood fiction." There never was any such place.

With the gradual decline of the Pope Valley mines, vehicle traffic thinned. There were good, faster and easier alternatives via Howell Mountain Road and Highway 29.

A quietude descended on the Oat Hill Road in the 1930s and 1940s. Emphasis turned to occasional recreational use by hunters on foot or horseback who wished to reach the backcountry. After World War II a new era of use emerged when the commercial manufacture of the jeep brought four-wheelers to challenge the grade.

By the 1970s the long-unmaintained Oat Hill was a serious challenge for a jeep. Enthusiasts called it the "best little four-wheelin' road in the state." Local jeep clubs made regular pilgrimages in long caravans from Calistoga to Aetna Springs or Oat Hill. They often did maintainance on the road. Trouble came mostly from those who were unfamiliar with the road and/or intoxicated. Several people were injured and killed at this time, usually on the exposed last rocky mile to the pass.

One of these accidents in 1973 involved a young man and woman and their infant child. The vehicle plunged 300 yards, turning over several times, killing the couple. The child was discovered hours later in good condition, still strapped to his jump seat about seventy-five feet from the wreckage. Accidents like these brought up liability issues for the County of Napa. After a number of hearings, the board of supervisors formally closed and abandoned the road in 1979.

This was seen as good news by preservationists, who ten years earlier had formed the Palisades/Swartz Canyon Project Committee. With Harry Tranmer as chairman, they envisioned the Palisades, including the Oat Hill Mine Road, as one day a part of Robert Louis Stevenson State Park. In 1969, 120 acres of land at the pass belonging to the Duff family was transferred to the Nature Conservancy, giving conservationists a legal foothold. This in turn was transfered to the Napa County Land Trust, which granted a public easement for many years. It is now owned by state parks. A 1988 bond act allowed the state to purchase the Table Rock property in 1993. Part of the dream had come to pass after twenty-five years, but even as local interests and state officials sought to use remaining funds for key land purchases, developers threatened to squash the dream.

Owners of a large parcel that includes Patrick Flynn's old homesteads proposed paving the Oat Hill Road and placing multimillion dollar ranchettes on hilltops. They attempted to regrade the road but were stopped by a vigilant Genji Schmeder, local Sierra Club leader. Undeterred, developers bought an easement to the north and in 1992 illegally bulldozed one and a half miles of road adjoining the Oat Hill Road. They did it without permit and without an erosion control plan, in flagrant violation of Napa County's Hillside Ordinance. The Board of Supervisors gave them a $5,000 fine, a mere slap on the wrist. Recommendations to remove the road and restore it to its natural state were not implemented.

In response to this threat, the Oat Hill Mine Trail Committee was born as a watchdog agency and advocate for the historic trail. It seeks to preserve the trail in its present state and permanently protect it as a state park. Constant community vigilance and support are needed to prevent development that would surely destroy this area.

Today, the Oat Hill Mine Trail is a locally popular hiking route with over 6,000 visitors a year. There may be no other like it in the world. Its unique geological and historical resources and obvious beauty make it richly deserving of preservation status. Efforts by many concerned people are helping to make this trail one to be enjoyed today and forever. You can join the cause by contacting the Oat Hill Mine Trail Committee, a part of Napa County Sierra Club, at P.O. Box 644, Napa, California 94559.

TRAIL NOTES*:

The hillside washout with part of a fence poised dramatically over it typifies the unstable soil encountered in the first ½ mile. The wide mix of trees include black oak, gray pine, toyon, scrub oak, and manzanita. Soon, Zahtila Vineyards (formerly Traulsen) appear downslope to your left. Silver dollar eucalyptus trees grow along the fence.

To your right is an old shale pit, actually weathered andesite lava. Similar rock ½ mile away was quarried for road base for Highway 29. Pass under a leaning oak tree at the fenced bypass that skirts one of the worst slope washouts on the trail. Here you get an idea of the wildflowers the Oat Hill Road offers in spring: brodiaea, fiddlenecks, buttercups, poppies and bush lupine. Watch out for giant poison oak bushes at the big switchback.

At ½ mile you see the worst slide of the 1995 flood, which stopped just short of taking out the trail. From here you soon enter rhyolite lava flows that occurred in the last stage of the Sonoma Volcanic field about three million years ago. The trail now faithfully follows the contours of the hills, meandering alternately into the shady stream canyons and out into the grassy meadows. You'll find the road builders one hundred years ago did a beautiful job. In places the trail seems too narrow to have accommodated freight wagons. Plant growth and some erosion have obscured the original width.

At mile 1 you can look straight down Lincoln Avenue, the main street of Calistoga. In another ⅜ mile is a clearing with large Douglas firs. Groupings of Indian warrior show here every spring.

A curious unit of rock around 1¾ miles confused earlier geologists into mapping it as sandstone. This fine-grained, white-to-tan-colored tuff fell as ash into an ancient lake during volcanic eruptions. Fossils are often found in

Geological information is taken from Trailside Geology of the Oat Hill Road *by Dean Enderlin.*

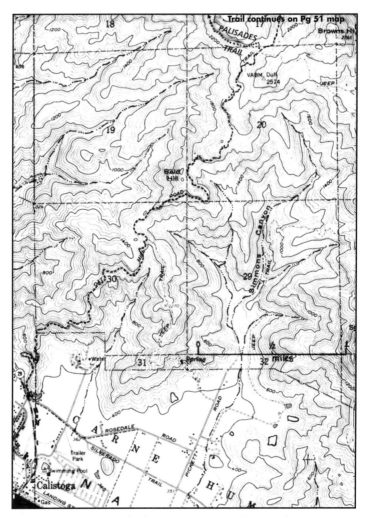

Trail continues on Pg 51 map

such water-lain rock, but not here. Violent volcanic eruptions of the time had virtually eliminated all plant and
animal life.

You pass a large meadow where Mamie Flynn lived
alone in a cabin. She got her water from the creek nearby
in spring, but in summer she walked to town and carried
it back in gallon jugs.

44

Just up the trail Mamie's father, Patrick Flynn, worked a mining claim from 1889 to 1907. He drove a crosscut one hundred feet into the hillside attempting to contact what he hoped was a deeply buried ore body. Ever the optimist, he claimed at various times to have struck gold, silver, or cinnabar, whichever was most in demand at the time. Probably not much came of it. Rock fall covered the entrance to the mine in the winter of '95-'96, rendering it inaccessible. At mile 2 the trail becomes rough and rocky, appearing bleached and iron stained. Chemical weathering through hydrothermal activity is the cause.

At 2¼ miles you meet a jeep trail junction. The southern portion appears on old USGS maps, but the northern part was cut illegally by landowners in 1992. In this area in fall or early spring you might see much sought chanterelle mushrooms. The variety of wildflowers continues with checker lily, hound's tongue, mule ears and nightshade.

The old wagon wheel ruts at mile 4

As the road surface becomes smooth at 2⅜ miles, the first of two scenic and steep grassy slopes appear. After the second field, an old erosion gully, enlarged dramatically by the March 1995 flood, has taken out part of the trail. Beyond, a hillside seep sports seepspring monkeyflower, yellow petals enclosing a red heart. It will flower into summer with enough water. No benches are found along the trail, but at mile 3 is a rock outcrop that has a perfect sitting dish, a good picnic/rest site with views way down into fir-shrouded Simmons Canyon. In this area, look for the first of many wagon wheel ruts. As you turn the corner, the Palisades burst into view. Vegetation changes from woodland and brush to open grasslands with few trees and much chaparral, reflecting a change in the type of volcanic rock. These lapilli tuff units are much coarser and indicate your approach to an eruptive center.

At 3⅜ miles you come to the distinctive and well-named Bald Hill. Geologically it is an andesite intrusive that has forced its way up through older rock. Along the base is an old dugout spring that once served as a watering hole for horses hauling freight wagons. If you feel energetic a detour to the crest of Bald Hill (state park property) is rewarded by one of the best views in the county. All of Napa Valley is visible from Calistoga to Napa, and to the north the entire stretch of the Palisades to Mount St. Helena.

Just past Bald Hill is a junction with a fire road, the route favored by jeepers in the four-wheel-drive days. Although in places a narrow corridor of buckbrush and ceanothus, the regular trail is much easier. The sweet lilac smell of white, yellow, and blue ceanothus flowers is for me the scent of California spring. After a stand of chamise, turn a corner for close-up views of Palisades outliers. On the road and cliffs are vitriophyres, chunks of black obsidian glass speckled white with feldspar crystals. They are encased in a matrix that once flowed as mud after torrential rains (geological term — lahar).

At mile 4 appear the best set of wagon wheel ruts on the west side of the Palisades, almost five inches at their deepest. The wooden wheels of freight wagons were capped with steel for protection. After many trips, ruts were formed in the relatively soft rock. The fire road shortcut joins the trail at a saddle. A smooth stretch of trail suddenly turns dramatic as it swings around a narrow turn, bordered by steep cliffs on one side and, on the other side, a dropoff

The Holm's place once stood at the summit of Oat Hill Mine Road

supported by stone buttressing built by Chinese labor. A rusting hulk of a vehicle lies half buried in brush, legacy of an unlucky driver.

For the next mile the trail is mostly solid rock, one reason a trip from the mines to Calistoga took all day. Mountain bikers will pay the price of their ambition on this stretch. Now the Palisades are directly in view. They are composed of volcanic mud flows, agglomerate and welded tuffs. It is here the volcanic eruptions were most violent. The Palisades are the upper layer of a series of step faults; the lower sets are seen at the base. Perched above are columnar andesite columns, much like the basalt columns at Devil's Postpile in the Sierra.

At 4⅞ miles you reach the trail's high point and enter the shade of oak/bay forest. At this unlikely but beautiful site, the Holm family homesteaded at the century's turn. A few antique-variety apple trees known as Arkansas Black are still bearing fruit in the orchard. Across from the orchard is the Palisades Trail junction. That trail climbs quickly past remnants of two stone houses and a barn, heading for the rugged cliffs above (see previous chapter). Directly up the

47

hillside from the ruins is a deep, round, fern-rimmed spring that was their water source.

From here you have three choices. One is to continue on the Palisades Trail to the Mount St. Helena trailhead. For those who prefer uphill to down this way is the better choice. It is 6 more miles and requires a car shuttle. Consider a ½ mile extension of your hike to reach the base of the Palisades, well worth it. The second choice is to continue east on the Oat Hill Mine Trail to its end, a satisfying completion of the old freight wagon road, passing through much more remote but equally spectacular country. This also requires a car shuttle but one requiring considerably more time. The third option is to return the way you came, 5 miles of steady downhill.

OAT HILL MINE TRAIL, EAST SIDE

Reclaimed route provides new gem of a trail

DIRECTIONS: From St. Helena drive one mile north on Highway 29, then turn right on Deer Park Road. Take Deer Park 8 miles to Angwin, then continue on North Howell Mountain Road to Pope Valley. At the Pope Valley Garage, turn left and go 3.5 miles to the Aetna Springs turnoff. It is one mile to the old resort, then 3.75 miles to the locked gate. The last 1.5 miles is gravel road.

DISTANCE: 3 miles one way to the Holm's place at the pass

ELEVATION GAIN: No net elevation gain, but plenty of up and down

GRADE: Moderate

BEST TIME: Winter, spring, fall

DOGS ALLOWED: Yes

INFO: Napa County Open Space District, 707/259-5933

SUGGESTIONS: This hike is the easiest way to the Palisades. For a greater challenge, place shuttle vehicles at the west and east ends for a shuttle hike of 8 miles.

TRAIL NOTES:

Step around the metal pipe gate. The County chose

this location in 1978 as the most appropriate to deter four-wheel drive vehicles when the road was abandoned. It never marked the end of the public road as some adjacent landowners thought. A short, uphill piece leads past the old Dey property on the right where a sign has the immortal but now almost illegible words, "trespassers will be turned into compost." The road is wide, rough and rutty now and soon leads to the junction with the Oat Hill Mine Road. To the right is the private Livermore Road. Our hike turns left, the road narrows, and at ¹/₅ mile you'll find the first definable wagon wheel ruts. Keep your eyes peeled for many more sites. A whitish rock hillside on the right is probably ash flow tuff, violently ejected from the earth at super hot temperatures. Due south is a view of Sugarloaf Peak, 2,988 feet, looking triangular from this vantage. The route runs between this peak and Twin Peaks to the north.

In summer this region can be witheringly hot and dry,

Deepest wagon wheel ruts on east side

but after a winter or spring rain the many seeps and small waterfalls, rivulets and creeks will make it an inviting rock garden. The roadside will be alive with wildflowers like California fuchsia, Indian paintbrush, Indian warrior, bush and seepspring monkeyflower, and several kinds of brodiaea: blue dicks, harvest brodiaea and Ithuriel's spear. To the south at ¹/₃ mile is a huge rock outcrop I call Armadillo Rock, with a massive overhanging top rock ridged like the armor plating on the animal's back. In the little valley

50

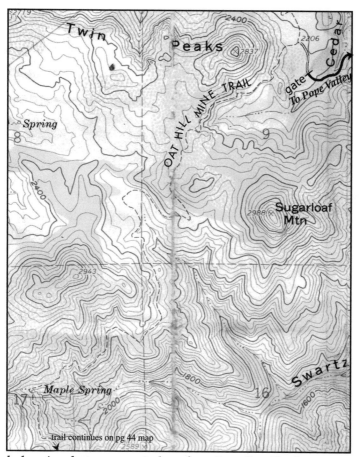

trail continues on pg 44 map

below is what appears to be a faux Standing Rock.

Before ½ mile you encounter what may be the best defined wagon wheel ruts on the entire Oat Hill. They are at least a hundred feet long, several inches deep and unmistakable. Beyond ½ mile you come to a beautiful piece of trail reminiscent of a Japanese landscape painting, a miniature gorge with a creek tumbling down into it, with mossy dark and dank nooks and crannies holding sedges, mosses, lichens, and stonecrops. A large oak seems to grow directly out of rock, and gray pines airily arch over the abyss. The creek

Hiker nearing the Holm's place

will sometimes overflow down old wagon tracks at a very sharp bend just beyond.

With some imagination, the wildly formed rock formations out here become an amusing identification game. The day of our hike I named two rock masses facing each other around ⅔ mile the Kissing Armadillos. My companion romantically commented they would forever be longing for each other but never consummate. Backing that up from the scientific viewpoint, I noted that with the inevitable effects of erosive weathering agents, they would indeed only be moving farther apart. After a creek crossing, you pass a cypress grove surrounded by knobcone pines. Then you encounter a confusing junction. The right fork looks more prominent but soon ends in brush. Take the left fork here. Notice more wagon wheel ruts, then crest a small hill. Pass by a road on the left, continuing straight and downhill now on rocky ground.

The top of the big U-turn beyond ⅞ mile presents a sweeping vista of rugged Swartz Canyon and the hills of Napa Valley. It has the look of a former target shooting area, with broken glass underfoot. Now make the 180-degree turn and head northwest along a highly erodable dirt cliff. These reddish tinted "badlands" are in places devoid of all plant life. At 1⅕ miles spin around the second 180-degree turn and head southeast. A two-foot high iron pipe cemented in stone at 1½ miles is the location of Pocai Spring, site of the old Rooker cabin circa early twentieth century. You soon will pass a large, accessible cave on the right.

The trail turns to parallel Swartz Creek at 1¾ mile. On a sunny day in spring the yellows, pinks, reds, and purples of wildflowers stand out brilliantly against the grays, browns and blacks of this rugged, rocky country. Enter a brush tunnel at 2 miles, cleared back or closing in depending on how recently trail work was done. You may wonder how ore wagons and six-horse teams got through here. This road was no doubt constantly maintained during the busiest mining years, but since then brush and detritus have narrowed it considerably. Come to a tight spot at 2¹/₅ miles however, with a cliff on one side and rock buttress work on the other, that was probably never any wider. The drivers were the best to be found.

Maple Spring was an important source of water for the teamsters and other travelers. Today, this is a BLM water reserve inholding. Beyond 2½ miles you come to a stretch of trail particularly shady and lush. On a north facing hillside, if your timing is right, you'll see a massing of lemon fawn lily (Erythronium citrinum), a beautiful, delicate nodding flower with six white petals and a yellow center, the leaves succulent green, mottled with brown. Ahead is a shady dell with bay, oak and buckeye and towering rocks half hidden by foliage and a tumbling cascade. Directly across the canyon is another large cave, and on the south ridge a chance to have more fun with fanciful rocks. Three curious rock forms caught my eye which in turns reminded me of a hound baying at the sky, a fancy twisted-neck gourd, and a bust of Barney Rubble. Then just before the end, I also saw a remarkable profile of W.C. Fields with his requisite bulbous nose. What do you see?

At mile 3 you come to the old Holm's orchard with four or five apple trees in a grassy meadow with baby blue eyes. This is a wonderful site for lunch as you ponder what life was like in this idyllic setting around 1900. You have three choices here, continue on the Oat Hill Mine Road to Calistoga (5 miles to end, see pages 37-48), turn right onto the Palisades Trail (6 miles to end, see pages 31-36), or return the way you came.

PETRIFIED FOREST LOOP

The only petrified redwood forest in the world

DIRECTIONS: From Calistoga drive northwest on Highway 128, turn left on Petrified Forest Road. Drive 3.5 miles to the entrance on the right.

HOURS: 10–5 every day in winter, 9-7 in summer. Closed Christmas Day.

FEE: $6 per person

DISTANCE: ½ mile. Wheelchair access for at least half the loop.

GRADE: Easy. Minimal elevation gain and loss.

BEST TIME: All year

INFO: Petrified Forest, 707/942-6667

SUGGESTIONS: A tour of the Meadow Trail happens every Sunday at 11 a.m or by request. The easy ¼ mile hike ends at a large ashfall area with an unrestricted view of Mount St. Helena. The peak provides a powerful visual reminder of the ancient volcanic explosion that flattened the redwoods here.

NOTE: Check out the enormous valley oak that stands in front of the gift shop. It is now well over 400 years old. From the size of this giant you can roughly calculate the ages of other large oaks.

Fifty million years ago the West Coast's climate was cooler and wetter, and redwood forests stretched from California to Alaska. Their range had shrunk by the time the Petrified Forest was buried three and a half million years ago. Researchers still debate the mechanics of its demise. Was it felled by a volcanic blast from the northeast, or did it fall on its own? If from a violent blast, different ash types suggest separate events rather than one.

Whatever the mechanism, the method of burial is clear. Thousands of years of eruptions buried the trees in rhyolitic volcanic ash. Silica, leached from the rhyolite by water, infiltrated the wood fibers as they decomposed cell by cell. The trees slowly petrified, literally turned to stone (petrifaction is from Latin, "turning to stone").

Gradual uplift of this site, combined with erosive weathering agents, had partially exposed some trees when they were discovered in the 1850s. They were left undisturbed for twenty years. Then a Swedish sailor, weary of the sea, settled here in 1871 to raise cows. After uncovering the redwoods while clearing his field, he realized their value as a tourist attraction.

Charlie Evans, known as Petrified Charlie, played host to Scottish author Robert Louis Stevenson in June 1880. Stevenson, writing in *The Silverado Squatters*, was more interested in the Swede than the ancient trees:

> And the forest itself? Well, on a tangled, briery hillside — for the pasture would bear a little further cleaning up, to my eyes — there lie scattered thickly various lengths of petrified trunk, such as the one already mentioned. It is very curious, of course, and ancient enough, if that were all. Doubtless, the heart of the geologist beats quicker at the sight; but for my part, I was mightily unmoved. Sight-seeing is the art of disappointment.

Evans sold the Forest following Stevenson's visit, and ownership then changed hands several times. Around 1910 it was bought by Frenchwoman Ollie Bockee (pronounced Bokay). Her excavations found several partially buried trees and included the tunnel that unearthed the Monarch. She built the ranchhouse in 1915, and the site's popularity soared. Aunt Ollie died in 1951, but ownership is retained by her heirs.

In 1978 the Petrified Forest was declared California Historical Landmark number 915. Since 1988 continuous upgrading, including new excavations and a new trail, has enhanced the Forest to welcome upwards of 75,000 visitors a year, at least a quarter of whom are from foreign countries.

TRAIL NOTES:

As you pass through the turnstile, look for a wooden arrow at the trailhead pointing toward a large chunk of petrified wood that you can touch and examine closely. Most of the ½-mile walk will be through a mix of evergreen forest — Douglas fir, madrone, live oak, gray pine — and chaparral species like toyon and manzanita. Ahead of you lie ten petrified tree or tree fragment sites.

The first site you come to is the Pit Tree, the only petrified pine tree among its stone redwood neighbors. In winter it may be partially submerged in water. This was part of the petrifaction process and does no harm. Employees sometimes use a high-power water spray to remove moss from trees without damaging the trunks.

Nearby is the Gully Tree. Long after burial and petrifaction, it broke into fragments through stress of gradual earth movement. The trail veers right and vegetation turns xerophytic briefly — scrub oak and chamise.

Just beyond a grassy meadow before ¼ mile is a collection called the Petrified Woodpile. From a bench one can contemplate a lifelike Lilliputian-scale model of a miner and his donkey representing Petrified Charlie and his companion standing beneath a grove of mature manzanita.

As the loop veers right again The Giant and The Queen lie close together. Each has its own viewing platform. The Queen is especially impressive. As if denying her own death and petrifaction, she has generated from her stone body a live tree. (Later on, note the 1911 photograph of The Queen in the gift shop. An auto is parked next to it. The young oak is noticeably smaller).

Ancient live oak beside the old ranch house

Next to the Queen lies a new excavation, unnamed as yet.

Halfway through your walk is the Monarch or Tunnel Tree, the largest in the Forest at 105 feet. Instead of removing an entire hillside, the tree has sensibly been excavated by tunnel. The public was once allowed inside but today, liability prohibits entry. A longtime employee informed me it is constantly caving in. The tree is actually better seen today due to improved lighting and removal of a fence.

The last tree on the loop is the Robert Louis Stevenson Tree. This is the one the Scottish author was so unimpressed with when shown by owner, Petrified Charlie. The trail begins its descent. You'll pass a bronze relief plaque of Charlie Evans with his pipe and Robert Louis Stevenson. Descend through magnificent old live oaks to the ranchhouse.

The Bockee ranchhouse has a fine, rustic, old-fashioned character about it. The pace is slower here and eases one back in time. Exit through the museum/gift shop. Both are well worth browsing. The geological display by Sonoma State professor Terry Wright is excellent. Pull up a chair at the library and read Elise Mattison's short article "California's Fossil Forest." Or browse through the visitor registers that go back to the 1940s. Some people have found friends' and relatives' entries from years back.

57

BOTHE-NAPA VALLEY STATE PARK

Napa Valley's most popular state park

DIRECTIONS: The park is halfway between St Helena and Calistoga on the west side of Highway 29.

FEES: $6 day use, $12-15 camping, For swimming pool: $3/adult, $1/child, 6 and under free.

BEST TIME: Spring, summer

INFO: Bothe-Napa Valley State Park, 707/942-4575

SUGGESTIONS: Bicyclists may use lower Ritchey Canyon Trail, and Spring Trail to the turnaround. Horseback riders can take advantage of a concession begun in 1995. A native plant garden used by the Wappo people is located next to the visitor center.

TRAILHEAD: At Horse Trailer parking lot, a short distance beyond the campground turnoff on the right-hand side. All trails begin here except the History Trail, which you will find by continuing to the end of the paved road paralleling the highway.

CAMPING: 50 family campsites, including 9 walk-ins. Water, restrooms, laundry, hot showers available. One group campsite holds up to 30 people. For reservations (recommended), call 1-800-444-PARK.

So much began here, so many pioneers are connected with Bothe Park, that it is like a history of the Napa Valley itself. Some highlights follow.

The Wappo people, closely related to the Coast Yuki of the northern Mendocino coast, occupied Napa Valley for at least four thousand years. They were composed of three tribelets, the northern Mishewal (Warrior People), the central Mutistul (North Valley), and the southern Meyahk'mah (Water Going Out Place). Each tribelet had mountain, valley and stream in their territory. Although they respected these boundaries, they practiced guardianship of the land rather than ownership.

The area we know as Bothe Park was home to the Mutistul Wappo, who had an encampment near Ritchey Creek known as Kaliholmanok. They would live here at various times throughout the year depending on factors like the weather and where the best food sources were to be found. The Wappo used and respected the full variety of the plant world, gathering plants for food, ceremony, technology (like basket making) and medicine.

Acorns, the staff of life, were gathered from the black oak and tanbark oak in fall to be made into soup, mush and bread. Bulbs of wild onion, brodiaea and Mariposa lily, known as Indian potatoes, were cooked or eaten raw. Shellfish and salmon, from the Napa River, and abundant game rounded out their diet. Blue elderberry was cut into split-stick rattles for ceremonial dance. Sedge and redbud were highly prized for strength and flexibility in basket making. The Wappo made baskets, a difficult skill to master, of all sizes and uses, including tight-weave baskets that were waterproof. They used yerba santa and angelica to cure many ailments, and sandbar willow bark like aspirin.

Traveling ancient trails, the Wappo people made an annual trek to Bodega Bay to trade with Coast Miwok for jewelry and clamshell bead currency. They also gathered and dried seaweed and salt to supplement their diet.

The thread of life the Wappo wove for millennia was unraveled in twenty short years, from 1836 to 1856. The Mexican government waged war on the Wappo, and white man's diseases weakened the tribe. Most devastating was the settlers taking of Wappo land, expelling the natives from their home. Some fled to the refuge of Li'leek near Clear Lake. Some blended into the culture. Between 1851 and 1856 the remaining 500 Wappo were bound and driven by United States troops to locations far from their ancestral lands.

Dr. Edward T. Bale, who some say survived a shipwreck on the Monterey coast, married into the Vallejo family in 1839. General Mariano Vallejo, commander at the Sonoma mission, granted Bale nearly 18,000 acres from Rutherford to Calistoga in 1841. Showing his sense of humor he named it *Rancho Carne Humana* (meaning human flesh), a play on

Bale's Grist Mill

Wheat replaced hide tanning as the number one industry in Napa County during the gold rush and continued to be important until 1890. Edward Bale employed pioneers Ralph Kilburn and Florentine Kellogg who built the mill by 1846. John Conn made the first millstones from material he found in the canyon behind the mill. The twenty-foot overshot wheel was powered by Mill Creek water brought in flumes originally made of dugout redwood logs. In the meantime the mercurial Dr. Bale got bitten by the gold fever and went to the Sierra foothills to prospect. By 1849 he had contracted, some say, a real fever and died that year in his adobe home off present Whitehall Lane. He left the mill and adjoining land to his daughter Isadora.

By 1853 Napa County was second only to Santa Clara County for wheat production in California. In fact, the only two grist mills north of San Mateo were the Bale Mill, and Chiles Mill in Chiles Valley. The original twenty-foot waterwheel was replaced by the present thirty-six-foot overshot wheel (meaning water sluices off the top), the largest historic wooden wheel of its kind in the United States. Isadora Bale, the early name Callojomanas. The controversial Bale was once publicly flogged by General Vallejo's brother, Salvador Vallejo, for alleged slander. Later Bale was convicted of attempted murder of Salvador but released for political reasons. Despite his faults, which included excessive drinking, he was a hard worker and made a shrewd business decision to build a grist mill (see "Bale's Grist Mill" below).

The golden age of settlement by American overland pioneers lasted nearly thirty years from 1841 to the coming of the railroad. Two of these pioneers who came to Napa Valley were Reason Tucker and Florentine Kellogg. Tucker and Kellogg made their way over the Great American Desert and into California in 1846. They missed being caught by the same Sierra snows that trapped the Donner party by only twenty-four hours. When Tucker heard of the Don-

later Mrs. Louis Bruck, built the Mill Pond in 1859 to ensure a steady supply of water for the mill. They sold Bale Mill the next year. Through the 1870s the Grist Mill (then the property of W.W. Lyman) was a successful business, and the granary served for dances, meetings and other social events. The wheat industry declined in the 1880s, but the Bale Mill continued intermittently as a custom milling operation until 1905 when it closed permanently.

W.W. Lyman continued the upkeep of the mill until his death in 1921. His widow, Sarah, sold it to the Native Sons of the Golden West soon after. The mill became a California State Historic Landmark in 1939 and two years later it was deeded to the County of Napa. In 1972 it was on the National Register of Historic Places and incorporated into the state park system in 1974. After a long restoration it was reopened in 1983. When the waterwheel, flume and gearing were restored in 1988, the wheel began turning again for the first time in 109 years. You can watch the milling operations most summer weekends and purchase genuine stone-ground flour.

ners' plight, he made four trips to rescue the survivors. He settled on a choice farm site on Ritchey Creek near present day Bothe Park. Some of his descendents still live in this area. In exchange for iron work on the Bale Mill, Florentine Kellogg received land on the south side of Mill Creek and built the oldest surviving frame house in Napa Valley, now owned by the Lyman family.

Historical firsts are plentiful here. In 1847 Sarah Graves Fosdick, widowed and orphaned by the Donner Party ordeal, opened the first American school in Napa Valley in a buckeye grove just across the road from the Bale Mill. At first it was a mere shelter of branches that allowed rain to pour in. This site is now in Bothe-Napa Valley State Park.

The White Church was also a first in Napa Valley, built in 1853 and named for preacher Asa White. The crude structure had separate seating for men and women. Tramps burned it down around the turn of the century. A plaque marks the spot in the woods near the park's picnic area. A stone's throw away is the Pioneer Cemetery, the first one in Napa Valley. Many of the Tucker family are buried here.

Both Reason Tucker and Florentine Kellogg would have been content to spend their old age in Napa Valley. Tucker and Kellogg had land holdings around the valley and Kellogg was active in local politics. But a claim to Tucker's land by Edward Bale's daughter, Isadora Bruck, went to the California Supreme Court. A contract with the previous owner was declared invalid, and Tucker lost everything in 1872. He moved to Santa Barbara to make a new life, as did Florentine Kellogg who was embittered by all the costly lawsuits against his friends and neighbors. Reason Tucker's son, George, married to Kellogg's daughter, remained in the valley. Their house is now used as headquarters for the state park. Tucker Farm Center and Tucker Road near the park recall the role played by the Tucker family in Napa Valley.

By the early 1870s two San Francisco families who bought country estates here ultimately were instrumental in the formation of the park. W.W. Lyman began to acquire

The Hitchcock barn, circa late 19th century

property in 1871, buying the Grist Mill and thirty acres for $10,000, mainly to protect water rights. Ultimately he owned 1,000 acres in this area. He moved into the house built by F.E. Kellogg in 1849 which is essentially unchanged today.

Dr. Hitchcock bought property in Ritchey Canyon in 1872, later building a summer home he called Lonely. Dr. Hitchcock is better known for his eccentric daughter nicknamed Firebelle Lillie. Besides chasing fire engines in San Francisco, one of her famous stunts was riding the train from Vallejo to Bale Station on the cowcatcher. The Hitchcocks planted orchard and vineyard on the hillsides and logged some trees. Most of the redwoods though had been cut by earlier pioneers. Drag lines used to haul the trees out by oxen later became hiking trails.

After Lillie Hitchcock Coit died in 1929, Reinhold Bothe bought 1,000 acres and developed his "Paradise Park." It eventually had forty-one cabins, eighty-six tent cabins, tennis and bocce ball courts, stables and a lodge. The swimming pool was built in 1941, still used today as an unusual feature of a state park. One casualty of that era was Lonely, burned in 1938. Reinhold Bothe's mother, the resident, was forced to jump from the flaming structure.

After several attempts to sell over the years, Bothe sold his place to State Parks and Recreation in 1960. The lodge was removed, but some cabins are used by park staff today. The swimming pool remains a popular summer attraction. In 1981, campers, once forced to endure the sound of traffic all night, were treated to a new remote campground with fifty sites, nine of the walk-in variety.

Today Bothe-Napa Valley State Park has 8½ miles of trails for hikers through one of the easternmost stands of redwoods in California. The rare and endangered Clara Hunt's milkvetch (*Astragalus clarianus*) is found in the park. Mountain lion, bobcat and rare bear sightings contribute to the park's wild nature. It has eighty-four species of birds including six kinds of woodpeckers, perhaps as many as when this was Native American land.

HISTORY TRAIL

DISTANCE: 1⅛ miles one way
GRADE: Moderate

TRAIL NOTES:

The wide path paralleling the highway soon leads to the Pioneer Cemetery. The site is undergoing a major restoration sparked by a 1997 state-sponsored study of the area by Jenan Saunders. Trees that were dropping limbs and damaging headstones were removed, to be followed by new interpretive exhibits along the path from the White Church to the cemetery itself. When complete, visitors will have a much fuller understanding of the vital historical role of the Tucker family, many of whom are buried here.

Signs direct you across the grounds to the base of a forested hill. The trail climbs steeply, flanked by young mixed forest of madrone, black oak, Douglas fir and tan oak. By contrast, down in the draw are magisterial old growth

Douglas firs. The trail levels at ¼ mile then climbs gradually. Very young trees seem to indicate orchard or vineyard once occupied this slope.

Soon you reach the high point. It's all level or downhill from here. Glimpses of hillside vineyard on Spring Mountain are seen to the west at ½ mile. Smooth claret-colored trunks of manzanita have grown into twenty- and thirty-foot trees. The best views to the west are before ¾ mile.

The trail descends to a crossing of a small tributary of Mill Creek. Watch for poison oak close to the trail. The terrain opens to oak and grassland at mile 1 and soon a side trail leads to Mill Pond. The stone dam was built in 1859 by Isadora Bruck, daughter of Edward Bale, and her husband, to store water to power the large Grist Mill wheel. You make a second bridge crossing and suddenly huge valley oaks appear draped with Spanish moss. Not even the buckeyes escape this beard-like epiphyte, a lichen sometimes called tree net.

The trail ends at 1⅛ miles at the historic Grist Mill (a visit is highly recommended). Across the creek from the Mill is the Lyman House, the oldest frame house in the valley. It was built from lumber cut in this canyon by Florentine Kellogg at the time of the gold rush. A large bridge across Mill Creek (always lush with redwood, spice bush and alder) leads to the parking lot.

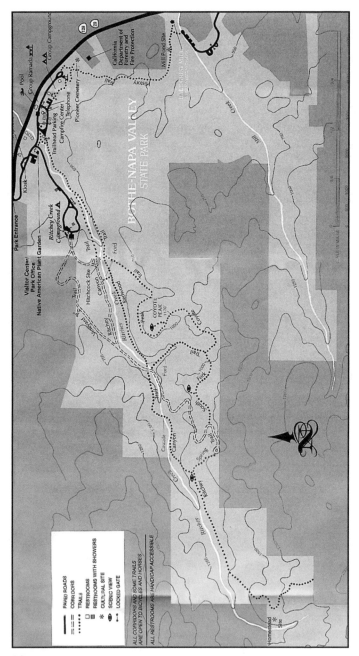

BOTHE-NAPA VALLEY STATE PARK

LEGEND

— PAVED ROADS
= = = CORRIDORS
• • • • • TRAILS
☐ RESTROOMS
▨ RESTROOMS WITH SHOWERS
✳ CULTURAL SITE
◉ SCENIC VIEW
•—• LOCKED GATE

ALL CORRIDORS AND SOME TRAILS
ARE OPEN TO BICYCLES AND HORSES.

ALL RESTROOMS ARE HANDICAP ACCESSIBLE

Park Entrance
Visitor Center/
Park Office
Native American Plant Garden

Ritchey Creek
Campground ▲

Kiosk

Pool
Group Campground
Group Ramada

Trailhead Parking
Campfire Center
Pioneer Cemetery
Telephone

California
Department of
Forestry and
Fire Protection

Mill Pond Site

History

Coyote Creek

Hitchcock Site

Redwood
Trail

Ritchey
Canyon
Trail

Ritchey

Ford

COYOTE
PEAK
1170

Coyote
Peak
Trail

South
Fork
Trail

Ford

Cascade
Canyon

Coyote
Canyon

Spring
Trail

Ritchey

Ritchey

Homestead
Site ✳

66

RITCHEY CANYON TRAIL

The longest hike in the park takes you to an old homestead

DISTANCE: 4⅛ miles one way
GRADE: Moderate

TRAIL NOTES:

Starting at Horse Trailer Parking, the trail parallels the access road, then crosses a paved service road. The trail is shaded by buckeye, maple, Douglas fir, madrone and black oak. Veer left at Ritchey Creek and join the gravel road at ¼ mile. The forest is now mainly redwood and fir, with thickets of spice bush more than ten feet tall beside Ritchey Creek.

After ½ mile is the Redwood Trail junction. Stay right at the sign, jumping from rock to rock at the stream crossing. This could be problematic at high water in winter and spring. A short side trail on the right leads to the campground. The prolific and invasive periwinkle (*vinca minor*) once growing so thick on the stream banks has been successfully removed by park personnel. Pass the campground on your right with the creek now on your left side. This stream is popular with kids in the summer who go wading and searching for crawdads. Related to lobsters, these crayfish are interesting creatures — they have eyes on movable stalks and can regrow their pincer hands.

At ⅞ mile is Lonely, once the summer home of the Hitchcock family. The Hitchcock house burned in 1938. In the 1940s the existing house was built and used as a gambling hall without the Bothe's permission. The stone fountain dates from the Hitchcock days as does the large redwood barn just uptrail. A side road to the right leads to the campground.

A short spur at mile 1 forks left across Ritchey Creek to the Redwood Trail. Riparian vegetation like blackberry, elk clover, thimbleberry and wild grape grow jungle-like in or near the creek. Several volunteer trails lead to more open sites by the creek, sometimes to small redwood groves thick with redwood duff underfoot. The pileated woodpecker is often seen or heard in this area, although it can be anywhere in the park.

Before 1¾ miles take the first trail junction to the right. To the left is Redwood Trail, and just beyond, Spring and South Fork trail junctions. Take Ritchey Canyon Trail and climb high above the creek then drop to meet it at almost 2 miles. Even on a hot day in a drought year, this site is cool. The water is cold and often a down-canyon breeze blows. There is a smooth rock in the stream on which to sit and cool your heels.

The trail climbs most steeply in the next ¼ mile, passing a spring-fed tributary of Ritchey Creek. Watch for dogwood flowering white in the spring and leaves turning pink in the fall. Trail surface around 2¼ miles is steep and loose. Above this section are two manzanitas up to twenty-five feet high and one foot in diameter. Scrub oak, toyon, bay and black oak reflect the drier slope.

A major trail junction at 2⅜ miles is unusual because of full sun exposure. You can see all of upper Ritchey Canyon to the west. Beyond is Diamond Mountain (2,375 feet). Peak 2,085 sits above a steep volcanic cliff to the northwest. Turn right to continue on Ritchey Canyon Trail and dive back into the forest. California Indian pink, also called catchfly, can be prevalent here in late spring.

Most of the redwoods you see in the canyon are second growth. The original redwoods were cut 150 years ago as the best building wood available. Just before mile 3 a shady moist spot under redwoods holds a patch of wild ginger. They have dark green, heart-shaped leaves with an indentation at the stem. If you are hiking alone, this area is quiet and isolated enough to bring to mind a quote by W.W. Lyman Jr. from his memoirs: *"I used to like to go where the trees were tall and close together and the underworld seemed alive with mysterious intimations."*

The next tributary stream crossing is exceptionally wide

for this canyon. Maple trees grow right in the creek bed. Around 3¼ miles you get a closer view of those volcanic cliffs on the canyon's north side.

Watch for an unmarked junction at 3½ miles leading to the Traverso homestead. A small trail leads across a creek through horsetail and vinca. Some vandal has taken the plating from a stone plaque remembering Sam Vance, who liked this site. A meadow on the steep hillside has an enormous fig tree roughly fifteen feet tall, twenty feet wide and fifty feet long. In the fall at least one of the apple trees in this old orchard has delicious fruit. This is a fine picnic site surrounded by redwood and fir. In the upper meadow coyote brush and pickeringia are slowly invading, but star thistle has already performed a hostile takeover.

Italians Biaggio and Margheritta Traverso built a home here in 1884. When the widow Margheritta filed for proof of homestead in 1890 she claimed the following improvements: a four room house, a barn, three cleared acres, one quarter mile of fencing, three quarters of an acre of grapes, and a few fruit trees for a total worth of 200 dollars. Later on, relatives of the well known Ghirardelli family of San Francisco bought this site.

To reach the trail's end, return to the unmarked junction and head uphill. The trail bends left and widens to a road, once the main access from Spring Mountain Road. Douglas fir, black oak, and tan oak predominate. You are allowed one view, as the forest thins, of Napa Valley and the Howell Mountains to the east. At 4⅛ miles a large yellow sign facing uphill marks the state park boundary. Just beyond is Ritchie Creek Vineyards. Return the way you came.

REDWOOD TRAIL

The easiest and most pleasant hike in the park

DISTANCE: 1 mile one way
GRADE: Easy

TRAIL NOTES:

The trail begins ½ mile up the Ritchey Canyon Trail. Veer left at the junction as the trail turns to a narrower dirt path. On the moist, north-facing slope sword ferns stay green into the droughty fall months. The invasive periwinkle (*Vinca major*) that used to cover the stream banks has been removed leaving the flood plain more natural.

As the terrain opens and becomes drier, Oregon oak appears. Pass the Coyote Peak Trail junction before ⅜ mile. A spur to the Ritchey Canyon Trail crosses the creek at ½ mile. From here bikes and horses are off limits. A goose pen of redwoods has five young trees in a circle twelve feet across, the progeny of a giant cut 150 years ago.

After a brief uphill climb look for star Solomon's seal in the spring. Usually seen singly or in small groups, at this site it covers the ground en masse. The trail climbs a narrow path beyond ¾ mile and traverses a steep, exposed hillside. There has been recent rerouting of the trail here and at the creek crossing at just before 1 mile. Ritchey Creek can be uncrossable in high water but usually it's an easy rock hop.

Redwood Trail ends at mile 1. Take Ritchey Canyon Trail back for a loop or continue on Coyote Peak or Spring Trails.

COYOTE PEAK TRAIL

An excellent and popular moderate loop hike

DISTANCE: 2¾ miles to peak or 4½-mile loop
GRADE: Moderate
DIRECTIONS: Take Ritchey Canyon Trail and Redwood Trail just over ¾ mile to Coyote Peak trailhead.

TRAIL NOTES:

Soon after commencing Coyote Trail look for a rock wall on the left. Beyond it is an old hillside vineyard site, planted by the Hitchcock family, with a few original redwood stakes. The trail then rises steeply through some tan oak and dogwood. In the next ¼ mile are several dead Douglas firs pockmarked with woodpecker holes. The flat-headed borer is a beetle responsible for many dead firs in this park.

Redwoods are usually seen in shady river canyons, but here around ¾ mile on the hillside just below a ridgetop are redwoods. Look trailside for flowering wild iris in the spring. Before mile 1 come around the shoulder of Coyote Peak for a splendid view of Ritchey Canyon watershed. At 1⅛ miles is a trail junction. Go left 500 feet to the summit. On the way you pass young redwoods on the south-facing slope, again defying conventional wisdom.

Once in the 1980s I arrived on top and was swallowed by an opaque thicket of trees. There was no view, no sense of having arrived anywhere. The careful clearing of some trees and brush has made this a more satisfying destination. Now you can see vineyards on Spring Mountain to the west, and Schramsberg Vineyards and winery to the north, with

Mount St. Helena beyond.

Return to the trail junction and turn left to make a loop hike. Follow a saddle, then, before sinking into Ritchey Creek watershed, you have a profile of Coyote Peak and Mount St. Helena on its left. Your descent is steep to a perennial creek just before 2 miles where springs nourish chain fern, thimbleberry, great thickets of spice bush and some of the finest redwoods in the park. Soon after is the South Fork Trail junction. Coyote Peak Trail ends here. Turn right and continue downhill on South Fork Trail to return via Ritchey Canyon, or turn left for more hiking.

ADDITIONAL TRAILS

SOUTH FORK TRAIL is 1⅜ miles long, starting near the four-way junction and ending on Spring Trail. At ¾ mile is a junction with Coyote Peak Trail and at about 1 mile it crosses a ridge between watersheds. At this point a short trail takes you to a view of the upper Napa Valley.

SPRING TRAIL is a ¾ mile continuation of the Ritchey Canyon Trail. At the four-way junction, cross Ritchey Creek and go steeply up the wide road past the South Fork junction and the springs that supply the park. The road ends in a circle turnaround where a narrower trail continues to the junction with Ritchey Canyon Trail.

VINEYARD TRAIL, ¾ mile long, starts at the back of the campground near walk-in site #31. The trail begins on a wide gravelled path, then veers right onto a dirt road after 200 feet. Around ¼ mile the trail/road continues as an easement through private property. After reentering the park, take the middle fork at the ½-mile junction and descend through chaparral, then forest to meet Ritchey Canyon Trail.

CEDAR ROUGHS WILDERNESS AREA

The world's largest genetically pure stand of Sargent cypress

Cedar Roughs has had little historical use. The rugged nature of this country and the dense cover of cypress and chaparral have discouraged both man and beast. Tentative mining explorations for mercury, magnesium, and chromite showed these deposits too poor for commercial venture. It is now managed by the Bureau of Land Management, which plans to keep its wild nature essentially unchanged. In 2006 Congress established the 6,350-acre Cedar Roughs Wilderness Area, which should ensure the area's protection.

By any standard, Cedar Roughs is an unusual wilderness. At first glance it may not seem as attractive as other places, but with familiarity the appeal grows. Its vast acreages of dense growth can be daunting considering its few trail miles. Yet, at the right time of year or the right time of day, Cedar Roughs is a place of rare beauty offering solitude and excellent wildlife viewing. Due to current access limitations and lack of public awareness, most visitors have been hunters during game season. With BLM trail expansion plans, hikers will soon find better opportunities.

This edition certainly offers more options at Cedar Roughs for hikers than the last one. Please note that the alternate hike in the second edition has been eliminated because BLM abandoned it, and no one seemed able to find it anyway! We now feature four new options including two best approached by some kind of watercraft.

73

They are, as you approach from the west: 1) Maxwell Creek, a ½-mile stroll alongside a perennial creek through a small, separate portion of the Roughs, 2) the main trail, a moderate mile hike to a pleasant oak-grassland meadow and views, 3) Old Pope Canyon Road, a wonderful hike along a stable old roadbed with no water crossings required, 4) the main boat-in access, a ½-mile hike to a secluded old hunting camp, and 5) Trout Creek boat-in access, a ½-mile jaunt above (or in, if you prefer) a perennial creek. Note that all but Old Pope Canyon Road require water crossings of some kind.

Rock outcrop on Pope Creek arm — experienced climbers only!

In fall 1871 J.J. Walters discovered three mineral springs off Pope Canyon Road, surrounded on the west, east, and north by steep hills, with a view south to what was then called Cedar Mountain. With partner J.W. Smittle, Walters made improvements to encourage summer visitors. The mineral waters were said to cure ailments like rheumatism, asthma and dyspepsia, and to ease heart disease. Daily stagecoaches brought the firm and infirm alike from Rutherford. Board and lodging at the hotel was $8 a week. Mineral drinking water was bottled and shipped from here by 1886.

Near the mouth of Trout Creek, where it empties into Pope Creek, Elisha Cornelius Samuels discovered his own springs in 1881. Samuels Springs was bought by G.R. Morris ten years later and became a first-class resort. In front of the large hotel, an enormous fountain served as the centerpiece for the resort, which had room for 150 people in cottages and tents. Morris provided a grass tennis court, croquet grounds and a dance hall for his guests' entertainment, while a dairy, a vegetable garden and a fifteen-ton capacity ice house provided for their needs. By 1901 daily mail and newspapers were delivered from Saint Helena. There was even a resident physician.

After World War I, these two resorts began a long, slow and genial decline. Samuels Springs was run as a rehabilitation camp for kids in the 1950s. After it was abandoned, Napan Bob McKenzie remembers the extensive vandalism he saw there on a visit in 1957. The damage included two pianos smashed to pieces, one a beautiful upright rosewood grand piano.

Walters Springs fared little better, staying open into the 1950s, run by a character named Mabel Wise. Vandals sacked most of the cottages after it closed, despite the fact that Mabel still lived on the property. Vacationers returned every summer for 25 years after it closed. In a 1981 interview, Mabel told how the mineral waters once cured her of a rattlesnake bite. Living alone so many years, she became resourceful and fearless. One night, hearing a clatter outside, she looked out her window and saw a bear looting her trash cans only inches away. She leaned over and kissed him!

A Marin architect in the early 1980s proposed to resurrect

Cedar or cypress?

Cedar Roughs should really be called Cypress Roughs. It contains the largest, genetically pure stand of Sargent cypress in the world. It is uniquely suited to the serpentine soil, but dry conditions in the upper elevations stunt these trees to ten feet creating a weird pygmy forest. Cedar Roughs is also unique for being the only known bear breeding area in Napa County. There is a small but stable population of about ten black bear.

Walters Springs as a modern health spa. Plans came to naught. In recent years, however, the property was purchased by Dr. Robert Jaffe and is now the Jaffe Institute for Spiritual and Medical Healing. Expansion plans include use as a day spa and as a year round spiritual retreat.

In 1980 Cedar Roughs was declared a Wilderness Study Area by BLM. Three years later it was designated an Area Of Critical Environmental Concern and a Research Natural Area. A final Environmental Impact Statement in 1986 recommended Cedar Roughs as unsuitable for wilderness designation.

Nevertheless, on October 17, 2006, President Bush signed into law the Northern California Wild Heritage Act, making Cedar Roughs federal wilderness. Its two separate parcels actually join at one corner, but for all practical purposes, egress from one to the other is not possible at this time. The western parcel of 160 acres can be reached via the abandoned Dollarhide Road along Maxwell Creek. The larger, eastern parcel can be reached 2.2 miles west of Pope Creek bridge (main entrance).

No trail now exists into the heart of Cedar Roughs but intrepid bushwhacking of about two miles will get you to the Sargent cypress groves. BLM is working on plans to build a trail to this highlight area.

MAIN ENTRANCE

DIRECTIONS: From Highway 29 or Silverado Trail north of St. Helena, take Deer Park Road northeast 8 miles to Angwin, then continue on North Howell Mountain Road over the summit to Pope Valley. Turn right on Pope/Chiles Valley Road and go 2 miles, then turn left on Pope Canyon Road. From the old Pope Valley airstrip, drive 6 miles. Look for the trailhead turnout on the right by a brown and yellow gate. There is an alternate entrance 0.1 mile west at a white gate that connects with the same trail.

DISTANCE: ⅞ mile one way

GRADE: Moderate

ELEVATION GAIN:	500 feet
BEST TIME:	Spring
DOGS ALLOWED:	Yes
INFO:	Call Bureau of Land Management, Ukiah office, 707/468-4000, or go to www.blm.gov/ca/st/en/fo/ukiah/cedarroughs.html for info and maps.
WARNING:	Winter and spring crossing will be cold and wet at best, dangerous or impossible in flood.
SUGGESTIONS:	When creek crossings are dangerous or unpleasant, take the alternate hike 1½ miles on the Old Pope Canyon Road (no crossings), which leaves from the same trailhead. On the west shore of Lake Berryessa is the Smittle Creek Trail, an easy 2½ mile jaunt. Entrances are at Smittle Creek Park and Oak Shores Park off the Knoxville Berryessa Road.

TRAIL NOTES:

Pass the brown and yellow gate and go downhill until the road curves left. Past a fence, turn right and follow the creek upstream on an old road. Soon you drop down on a steep path past wild grape and willows, then follow the creek where bay, scrub oak, manzanita and gray pine grow. At ¼ mile drop to the creek to find cottonwood and alder.

The trail lies across the creek as you stand under a large rocky outcrop with a lone, bent gray pine near its top. In fall you will find a dry crossing through willow thickets but during high water, wading will be necessary. I like to have sandals for crossing and stash them on the other side for the return. Take the path uphill to where another path joins, then cross a streamlet with double outlet pipes. On the left you'll see a collapsed wood and corrugated metal structure that was reportedly a goat pen. In summer and fall the grasses hold thousands of tiny white hayfield tarweed flowers.

Above the ruins is a shallow depression in a field (dry when I saw it) that looks like an old stock pond. The trail turns left and heads uphill and soon the width will narrow due to overgrowth of ceanothus, manzanita and toyon. As you ascend a panorama of Pope Canyon emerges, with the white buildings of Walter Springs behind you. At ²/₃ mile you meet a confusing junction. The left fork is simply a hunter trail that goes nowhere. Stay on the main road as it takes a sharp right, then turns rutted and stony. Berryessa Peak at 3,057 feet comes into view with its radio and microwave towers but now missing its fire lookout, which burned in the 2004 Rumsey Fire.

After ¾ mile the ascent eases and the trail drops slightly to an old jeeper's camp among blue oaks. On the far hillsides in

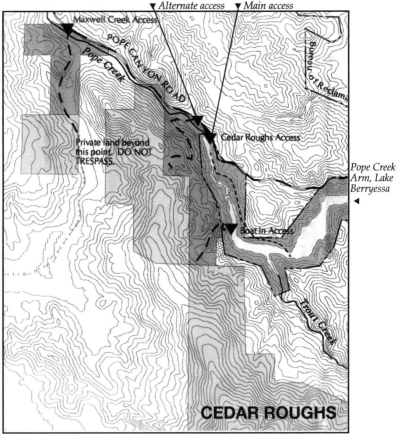

Cedar Roughs W. A. extends 3½ miles south

spring redbud stands out in a blazing magenta color against the gray greens of the chaparral. Several options allow further exploration. The first is a track from the meadow heading left toward an obvious ridgeline. This, if you're brave, will lead to the stand of Sargent cypress for which the Roughs should be named. It is a serious bushwhack as of this writing. However, Bureau of Land Management has plans in 2007 to not only improve the existing trail but develop a new extension for about ¾ mile toward the main Wilderness Area. Your second option is to continue on the main trail, happily wandering through oaks and grass hemmed in by the barrier chaparral. It wanders down and to the right. If you find the path of least resistance, you'll easily come to an overlook at a private property boundary. Down below is Maxwell Creek, the old Dollarhide Road and the pastoral Monahan ranch.

Your third option (recommended) is to ascend the "Viewpoint" from the meadow. If you are at all good at route finding, there will be no bushwhacking to the modest summit at 1,042 feet. The 360-degree view is superb: Lake Berryessa, Cobb Mountain, Mount. St. Helena, Sugarloaf and the back of the Palisades over Calistoga, all of Trout Ridge in the Roughs, Samuels Springs and Pope Canyon Road. Note how remarkably level is the three-mile ridgeline from Three Peaks to Angwin. From here, return the same way.

OLD POPE CANYON ROAD

Even though this is an alternate route, it is the most obvious and easy to follow hike in the Roughs area. It is an easy and pleasant hike used by few people. It is slightly downhill on the way out but elevation gain on the return is minimal. This hike features spring wildflowers, outcroppings of serpentine and slate, and fine views of Pope Creek and the Pope Creek arm of the lake.

DIRECTIONS: Same as for the main access to Cedar Roughs
DISTANCE: 1½ miles one way

GRADE:	Easy
ELEVATION GAIN:	Negligible
BEST TIME:	Spring, winter (no creek crossings)
DOGS ALLOWED:	Yes
WARNING::	Even though confusingly a "No Firearms" sign is displayed at the entrance, Cedar Roughs is a Type C hunting area as defined by the Department of Fish and Game, meaning no permits, passes or reservations are required. However, it is unlawful to shoot within 150 yards of any developed site or dwelling and from or across any road or trail. Hunters may hunt during designated seasons. Turkey season is usually April-May and deer season is September-October but check with California Dept. of Fish & Game for exact times.
SUGGESTIONS:	Take a picnic lunch with you and lounge under shady oaks at trail's end. Bring your swimsuit when weather is nice.

TRAIL NOTES:

The trail starts at the brown and yellow gate with adequate parking. After the gate you'll pass a map dispenser, likely with no maps in it. Follow the old road as it curves left to parallel Pope Creek. Blue oaks and gray pines shield wildflowers like baby blue eyes and frying pan poppies. Outcrops of soapstone and slate (some pencil slate) on the left tumble down to litter the old roadbed. Skirt a washout at a small tributary just before ¼ mile. This is a rough access to the creek itself and the hike to the main boat-in access (see page 83). The Lake Berryessa area is a haven for birdlife. Here on Pope Creek you may see a wide variety such as mallards, herons, turkey vultures, Canadian geese, western grebes, hawks, eagles, both bald and golden, and osprey.

Beyond ⅓ mile the creek will start to metamorphose under the influence of Lake Berryessa. A huge, photogenic outcropping of rock narrows the canyon, forming a deep pool at its base before the lake arm really widens for good. Just beyond the rock outcropping is a side trail that leads to a road ending at the lakeshore. For much of this hike you are shielded from Pope Canyon Road by a hillside and will find it's remarkably peaceful and quiet here despite the roads' proximity and motorcyclists' penchant for speed. At $^2/_3$ mile is a side road leading to the lakeshore. Soon you'll see an old road slicing the hillside across the lake arm in two big switchbacks. This is the boat-in access trail. Pass through the opening in a diagonal fence line at $^4/_5$ mile, demarcating the boundary between Bureau of Reclamation and Bureau of Land Management properties. The road curves left through an old road cut, and the views really open up. You can see the canyon of Trout Creek and its confluence with Pope Creek and above that the ruins of Samuels Springs Resort (binoculars helpful).

At one mile you reach an inviting meadow with five black oaks. Pass through another diagonal fence line and the road narrows to trail. A glittering hillside of serpentine leaves its shiny smooth tumbledowns on the road. Just before 1½ miles the road abruptly ends in the lake, next to a bank of rounded sandstone boulders. Here is another, larger meadow with

Classic Chevy Bel Aire on Pope Canyon Road

oaks, perfect for picnicking but watch for rattlers in spring and summer. You may see and hear fishermen talking as they troll for bass. Someday there will be a continuation of the trail along the north lakeshore to connect near Pope Canyon Bridge.

MAXWELL CREEK ACCESS

DIRECTIONS: Take Deer Park Road north of St. Helena about 6 miles to Four Corners, where Old Howell Mountain Road and White Cottage Road meet. Deer Park Road has become North Howell Mountain Road. Continue 2 miles to Angwin, then into Pope Valley. At the old Pope Valley Garage, bear right on Pope/Chiles Valley Road, then left on Pope Canyon Road. From the old Pope Valley airstrip, drive *exactly* 4.6 miles to the trailhead. Do not follow the Bureau of Land Management website directions from here, because they overstate the distance by exactly one mile. Locate a wide turnout on the right with a large, crescent-shaped berm and park there. The trailhead is found at a rusty gate on the west end of the turnout.

DISTANCE: Slightly over ½ mile one way

GRADE: Easy

ELEVATION GAIN: Negligible

BEST TIME: Spring

DOGS ALLOWED: Yes

WARNING: Winter rains make Pope Creek dangerous to cross. Cedar Roughs has long been popular with hunters. Turkey season is April-May, deer season is September-October.

TRAIL NOTES:

The hike starts at the beginning of the old Dollarhide Road. Head down to the creek, passing under, over or around a big downed tree. Wade the creek using your favorite water shoes you've brought just for this purpose. When I crossed, there was pink marker tape on a willow on the *opposite* side.

You might leave your crossing shoes to dry by an oak on the far bank. The road takes you up and left to parallel Pope Creek for a brief stretch, then veers right to follow Maxwell Creek on its west side.

The road is in pretty good shape other than a bad washout here and there. You will pass some leather oaks, a low and bushy, somewhat rare species adapted to serpentine soil. In spring, white ceanothus is conspicuous and aromatic. At $^1/_3$ mile a deeper part of Maxwell Creek has seen use as a swimming hole. Here, a wood crossbeam high up in two alder trees has been secured and a rope attached to the middle for use as a rope swing. You soon pass over a small tributary. As the canyon widens a bit, the larger and unfortunately separate part of Cedar Roughs comes into view. The part of the Roughs you are in is an 'island' property of BLM.

After passing some more erosion gullies on the creek side of the trail, you come to a fence and the end of this short excursion after ½ mile. Dollarhide Road continues as private property. Please respect private property rights. Turn back here and return the same way.

BOAT-IN ACCESS

DIRECTIONS: Same as for Main Access to Cedar Roughs

DISTANCE   From main gate: one mile one way. Boat-in access: ¼ mile one way.

GRADE: Moderate, some cross-country, rough ground, brushy

BEST TIME: Spring

DOGS ALLOWED: Yes

INFO: Call BLM, Ukiah office, 707/468-4000, or go to www.blm.gov/ca/st/en/fo/ukiah/cedar-roughs.html for info and maps.

SUGGESTIONS: Be prepared for variable conditions, seasonal fluctuations in water levels, and cross-country hiking. Consider paddling in from Lake Berryessa, or launching a small, portable raft from Pope Creek arm.

TRAIL NOTES:

Start at the main access to Cedar Roughs then follow the Old Pope Canyon Road for about ¼ mile. At a prominent washed out gully, carefully climb down to the creek. The best crossing we found was a few hundred yards downstream where the canyon narrows. At low water this is a rock hop (dry) crossing or easy wade. It may not be accessible at all during high water. Continue along the other shore until coming to a prominent rock outcrop. At low water it is fairly easy to rock scramble between the rock and the creek. Some rough bushwhacking around the prominence may be necessary during high water. Continue downstream along grassy slopes, sometimes steeply angled. Before one mile you arrive at an old road. It is almost directly opposite a side road access to Pope Creek off the Old Pope Canyon Road.

There are some old wooden boards near the start. Follow the old road for slightly more than ¼ mile, sometimes around encroaching brush. When you come to a stream with an old wood platform you are close. Just up ahead is an attractive grassy meadow with large blue oaks. You will see some interesting old junk scattered around that includes several steel spring bed frames (indication of a hunting camp), rusting machinery, and remains of fences. In a shallow depression is a perennial flowering bulb, evidence perhaps of more permanent habitation at one time. At the perimeter of the meadow are two dumpsites filled with old tin cans. Likelihood of solitude at this peaceful spot is high.

BOAT-IN ACCESS AT TROUT CREEK

DIRECTIONS: See Cedar Roughs main entrance

DISTANCE: The hike is ½ mile one way, approach by boat is one or two miles

GRADE: Easy

ELEVATION GAIN: 150 feet

BEST TIME: Spring, summer

DOGS ALLOWED: Yes

INFO: Bureau of Reclamation, 707/966-2111

SUGGESTIONS: You have several options for reaching this trail. One option is to launch your kayak or canoe from Putah Creek Resort, a short distance north on the Knoxville Berryessa Road from its junction with Pope Canyon Road. A parking fee is required. If your boats are portageable, launch from near the Pope Creek Bridge. Or if they are light and/or inflatable, start at the main entrance to Cedar Roughs, walk ⅓ mile and find the access road just past a major rock outcropping and a gentle descent to the Pope Creek Arm of Lake Berryessa.

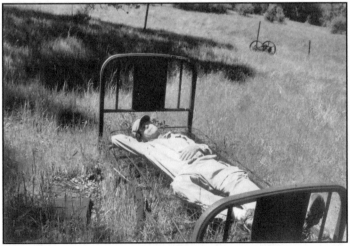

A hiker reclining at the trail's-end meadow

WARNING: Be aware that power boaters use this water-way also.

TRAIL NOTES:

A spit of land projecting from the mouth of Trout Creek is your hike's starting point. Follow the west shore for almost ⅛ mile then pick up the old grassy track gently rising from the creek. This distance may vary depending on lake level. At ½ mile the road splits, the left fork shortly ending in a steep, massive land slump. Take the right fork uphill, then down as the track winds past oaks and gray pines. It's fun to imagine the old days when visitors took this same road by horse-drawn wagon to spend a week or month at the private, now defunct Samuels Springs Resort. The trail ends before ½ mile at private property.

LAKE BERRYESSA'S NORTH END TRAIL

DIRECTIONS: From Highway 29 north of St. Helena, take Deer Park Road to Angwin, continuing on North Howell Mountain Road, negotiating the

Canoeing into Trout Creek on the Pope Creek Arm of Berryessa

steep Pope Grade into Pope Valley. Turn right on Pope/Chiles Valley Road, taking the second left (first is Barnett) at Pope Canyon Road. From the junction at the old airstrip, turn left and follow Pope Canyon Road to the Knoxville/Berryessa Road junction and turn left. Follow Lake Berryessa's west shore and cross the Putah Creek arm. Just after the bridge, park at the second turnout on the right, the trailhead for the North End Trail. You will see a trail sign and map dispenser.

DISTANCE: 2½ to 4 miles one way depending on route

ELEVATION GAIN: Negligible

BEST TIME: Spring

DOGS ALLOWED: Yes

INFO: Bureau of Reclamation, 707/966-2111

WARNING: At this time the trail is discontinuous but is slated for realignment and rebuilding soon. Be prepared to do some easy cross-country hiking. There is really no way to get lost because your parameters — the road and the lakeshore — are so close together. Wear long pants for thistly meadows and watch for ticks in the wet years. Rattlesnakes may be around, usually in April and May.

SUGGESTIONS: Do as long or as short a hike as you wish. You may exit the trail at virtually anytime as most of the eleven access trailheads have a feeder trail. A shorter hike may be done by avoiding the loop trails around the peninsulas, but these detours often have the best scenery and wildlife. A round trip hike could easily be done in a day, or if you choose to go one way, a car shuttle may be arranged by placing vehicles at either end of the route. If you are alone you could stash a bicycle at one end (lock it up here) and have the option of riding back along the pleasant and lightly traveled road. Remember your binoculars!

TRAIL NOTES:

The North End Trail is a surprisingly rewarding jaunt. It has many habitats to walk through, splendid views of Blue Ridge and Lake Berryessa, phenomenally varied and prolific bird life, and all this on a trail little used! You will see fishermen close to the access points, but other than that and boats going by, you will see few people on this trail. Sure, you're sandwiched in between a road and a lake with motorboats, but think positively and these become attributes. You'll find so much of interest here that all of it can be enjoyed together.

On the hike I did (after the fourth driest winter on record), I passed through scented pine forest, a grove of shady old toyon shrubs, tall green grassy meadows with ancient valley oaks, and lunched under a picturesque grove of blue oaks on a peninsula that led to a large, dying oak hosting at its top a massive osprey nest with both of its residents at home. One gratifying observation I made was seeing hundreds of tiny blue oak seedlings. The regeneration of blue oaks is problematic statewide, but here they are reproducing well. Despite the light winter rains, I saw many wildflowers, including blue-eyed grass, masses of wild vetch humming with honey bees, the wonderfully named, dandelion-like blow wives, large showings of Ithuriel's spear, deep purple wild iris, Chinese houses, lupine, and the exquisite tidytips (Layia platyglossa), with its yellow center and white tips.

For birders, Lake Berryessa may be the best place in the county. On this day I saw raucous Canadian geese, heard the sweet song of meadowlarks, saw one bald eagle hanging out Buddha-like in a gray pine, and spotted haughty blue herons, three osprey (very common and easy to see) and the ubiquitous wild turkey, plus numerous LBBs (little brown birds) my birder friends can tell you more about than I.

About ¼ mile in you will pass a rocky, wooded island that may hold some interest for scramblers. Often you'll see fishermen as you pass above the inlets. Motorboats or jet skiers roar by but leave in their wake the gentle lapping of waves on the shoreline. Homesteads on the far eastern shore can clearly be seen under the towering scarp and rim rock of Blue Ridge, its high point culminating in Berryessa Peak at 3,057 feet. Take your time on this walk, stroll or saunter as John Muir used to say, find some ideal picnic site on a bluff overlooking the lake, take a nap and enjoy the serenity this part of Napa County has to offer.

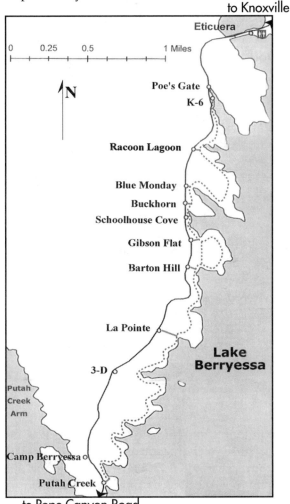

LAKE HENNESSEY

Superb waterfowl viewing in winter

DIRECTIONS: From Saint Helena drive east on Pope Street to Silverado Trail. Cross the Trail at a diagonal onto Howell Mountain Road. When Howell Mountain veers left, continue straight on Conn Valley Road to the northwest corner of the lake. The west side trail begins before you reach Greenfield Lane. Drive another mile along the lake to a locked gate to reach the east side (main) trailhead. Bikes must turn back here.

HOURS: One hour before sunrise until sunset

DISTANCE: 2 miles one way

GRADE: Easy, with minimal elevation gain or loss

BEST TIME: Winter, early spring

DOGS ALLOWED: On leash

SUGGESTIONS: The picnic area at the base of the dam, off Highway 128, is open weekends from Memorial Day to Labor Day. It has shade trees, tables, restrooms, water and a ballfield.

Irishman John Conn came to California in 1844 by way of Illinois. During construction of the Bale Mill in 1846 he took rock from a nearby hill and fashioned the first millstones. His claim to 6,000 acres of valley and mountain land east

The trail along the lakeshore

of Saint Helena was never formally granted by the Mexican government. He lost his land in the valley named for him and died in Napa, by one account, due to excessive drinking. His nephew, Connolly Conn, settled in Conn Valley in 1855.

In the mid-1880s work was begun to connect Rutherford and Monticello (in Berryessa Valley) via railroad. According to authors of a *Saint Helena Star* news article, the San Francisco and Clear Lake Railroad had cleared right-of-way on lower Sage Canyon skirting Conn Valley, then through steep upper Sage Canyon to Chiles Valley Road. By 1887 all work had been abandoned, with equipment like wheel barrows scattered where thrown.

The pastoral simplicity of Conn Valley remained unthreatened until World War II made Napa a commuter town for Mare Island Naval Base. Milliken Dam no longer supplied enough water for Napa's growing population, so the city bought 2,600 acres in Conn Valley in 1942. Conn Valley had several farms of apple orchards and grazing land. It's reported that the soil was not rich and was cultivated sparsely.

Work on the earthen dam began in 1945 after a summer

of clearing the land of trees and farm buildings. It took only six months, using impacted water-impervious clay materials and rocks of all sizes, to build the dam 110 feet high and 200 feet thick at the base. It holds back 33,000 acre-feet of water from Conn, Chiles, Sage and Moore Creeks, sixteen times the capacity of its predecessor, Milliken Dam. Edwin R. Hennessey coordinated Napa's water development for many years. The city council named the lake for him in 1951.

Engineers discovered a design flaw in 1963 when a wet winter caused the spillway to overflow and undercut Highway 128, closing the road. A concrete plug called an Australian Baffle was installed to divert the flow. Since then it has been a popular spectacle for locals to watch. During lake overflow, tons of water come churning down the channel at freeway speed, crash into the baffle with deafening booms, and create a geyser dozens of feet high. In the 1986 flood, fallout drift spray from the geyser was so heavy that drivers drove blind for a short section as windshield wipers slapped uselessly.

Fishing, boating and wildlife viewing are popular today with a new boat launch facility installed in 1990. The picnic site at the base of the dam is open weekends from Memorial Day to Labor Day.

In winter Lake Hennessey is one of the best places in Napa County for viewing birds, especially waterfowl. A short list of birds one might see in a few hours would include: mourning dove, bluejay, American robin, red-winged blackbird, yellow warbler, meadowlark, junco, flicker, red-headed woodpecker, starling, seagull, crow, turkey vulture, kestrel, kingfisher, red-tailed hawk, Cooper's hawk, northern harrier, blue heron, mallard, coot, Canadian goose, pelican, cormorant, bald eagle, golden eagle and osprey.

TRAIL NOTES:

Take the right fork past the metal gate (left goes into private property) over a small creek to a sign making sure

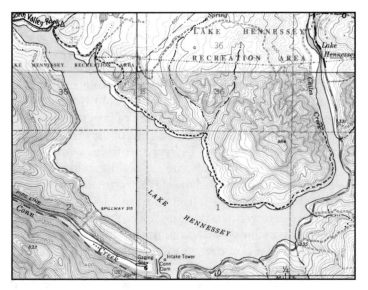

you know Lake Hennessey is the water supply for the city of Napa. Swimming or any acts of pollution are forbidden. Another fork in the road appears. Take the right one past another locked gate. Depending on the season, the lake may be right below the road or hundreds of feet away.

A mature gray pine forest stands on the left before ¼ mile. It is no coincidence that road cuts below it show grey-green shiny rock known as serpentine. Magnesium-rich serpentine soil is toxic to most trees, but gray pines love it. The day I went through, piles of pine cones lay below the trees, stripped clean of their tasty nuts by gray squirrels.

Lakeside, a tree stump is a favorite perch of the great blue heron. They are graceful flyers, holding their heads in close to form a U or S shape in the neck, while flapping wings evenly. Tall reeds nearby are great habitat for smaller birds.

Pass under oaks draped with Spanish moss at ¼ mile. Top a small hill and as the road heads downhill, hillside vineyards on Pritchard Hill come into view to the southeast. The hills across Lake Hennessey are clothed in oak woodland or dense, mixed evergreen forest, while more exposed nearby slopes have chaparral or blue oak/gray pine. In the spring, masses of Ithuriel's spear and soap plant bloom among the grasses.

Just before ½ mile the road levels out and terrain is flat and open for the next ⅓ mile. This is a likely place to see the kestrel (sparrow hawk). The small, colorful falcon can be seen hovering over fields in search of prey. Sounds may carry far on a calm day. Conversations of fishermen far out on the lake can sometimes be heard word for word.

Across the lake at ¾ mile you can see the spillway, and to its left the intake tower and the earthen dam itself. The road begins a big swing to the left, circling an inlet bay, a favorite place for waterfowl to congregate. Large numbers of Canada geese, coots, mallards and other ducks stop here.

A small, flat boulder on the left makes a fine resting bench at ⅞ mile. The creek crossing at mile 1, flood-damaged since 1996, has been repaired. The gap was cleverly bridged with a recycled Union Pacific railroad car. At the hilltop a small grove of Spanish moss-draped blue oaks seems like a tropical island compared to the flat, open terrain on either side. Drop down and to the left off the hill, passing under one of the larger blue oaks and into the open.

Before reaching the next tributary at 1½ miles, look northeast to a fine hillside of oak crowned with gray pines. In a wet winter, you may be lucky enough to spot a bald eagle or two perched in one of these pines. If you have never seen one, his great white head is unmistakable.

On a clear day, look to the northwest past Angwin where only the tops of the north, south and middle peaks of Mount St. Helena will be visible. Spring Mountain west of St. Helena is also visible through a gap. The trail skirts the hillside past the creek, and as you turn left (east), traffic on Highway 128 will become noticeable.

At 1¾ miles the trail orientation turns once again to the north. The road rises higher above the lake passing under live oaks. Some pine trunks and even fence posts are riddled with acorn woodpecker holes, many filled with acorns. The

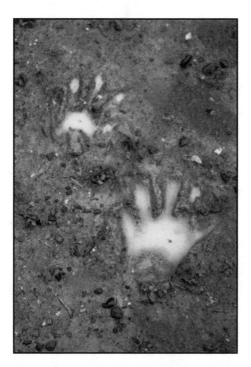

road now dips and twists through superb oak woodland.

The new boat launch facility comes into view across the lake. The road then dives and climbs to a gorgeous live oak-studded hilltop. To the southeast is a close view of Pritchard Hill and Chapellet Vineyards. At mile 2 you come to a locked gate and trail's end. A social trail leads downhill past some fruit trees, often an indicator of old homesteads. It ends in about ¼ mile. Return the same way.

RECTOR RIDGE TRAIL

Fast track to valley views

DIRECTIONS: From the intersection of Trancas Street and Silverado Trail in Napa, drive north on Silverado Trail 8 miles to Yountville Cross Road, then 0.7 mile more to the County of Napa's Maintenance Facility at 7292 Silverado Trail. It is just south of the Dept. of Fish and Game entrance. A turnout for several cars is on the east side of the road.

HOURS: Dawn to dusk

DISTANCE: ½ mile one way

GRADE: Moderate

BEST TIME: Winter, spring

DOGS ALLOWED: Yes

ELEVATION GAIN: 700 feet

INFO: California Department of Fish and Game, 707/944-5500

WARNING: Archery hunting of deer and wild turkey is allowed at various times from spring through fall.

At 1600 feet in elevation east of Yountville in the mountains named for Isaac Howell lies the valley of Foss, source for Milliken and Rector Creeks, two important early water sources for Napa and vicinity. Most of the smaller, satellite valleys east of Napa Valley are named for early settlers such as Pope, Conn and Chiles. One might assume a connection between Foss Valley and the legendary stage coach driver Clark Foss of Knight's Valley, but historical research so far indicates this is not the case. Foss Valley remained unsettled during the Mexican era although placer mining probably took place. Wheat growing and stock raising began in the 1870s and viticulture was established by 1881. The largest land owners by 1900 were Moser, Dickey and Varty (the Moser ranch is now Atlas Peak Vineyards, and the cattle and horse ranch of the latter two is now the Circle-S Ranch). By the early 1890s phyloxera was ravaging a good part of Napa Valley, but curiously Foss Valley was never affected. Grape growing continued undisturbed here, it is thought, due to its isolation and the relative low humidity of its microclimate.

Foss Valley wine growers took their grapes to the Borreo winery in Soda Canyon in the late 19th century and by the early 20th century were transporting them all the way to the Migliavacca winery in downtown Napa. The conversion from grapes to other fruits that occurred in Napa Valley during Prohibition also took place in Foss Valley. A gradual return to grapes after the 1950s is now complete and absolutely dominates this somewhat unknown upland valley.

Southwest of Foss Valley, a soda springs was discovered in 1855. A hotel was built soon after, but it was Colonel J.P. Jackson who made a world class resort of Napa Soda Springs in the 1870s. San Francisco's wealthy would escape the city fogs to visit for a week, a month, or a whole season, relaxing, enjoying the warm climate and many activities like swimming, horseback riding and dancing at night in the great Rotunda. Its international reputation brought 23rd president Benjamin Harrison to visit in 1894. Colonel Jackson was the first to see the economic windfall in bottling and marketing mineral water and thus pioneered the bottled water industry in this country. With the automobile, America's vacation habits became mobile and long summer stays grew out of fashion. World War I, the Depression and devastating fires were other factors in its eventual demise.

At the north end of Foss Valley stands Atlas Peak (2,663 feet), named by A.V. Evans for the Greek god who held the world on his shoulders. His resort was given a boost when the 1880 Committee Report on a Proposed State Hospital for Consumptives was published. It found that Atlas Peak and specifically Evans resort was the single most ideal site for a tuberculosis hospital in the state of California. Its moderate climate and situation above the valley fogs made it perfect for all patients with lung ailments. Although the hospital was never built here (it went to Weimar, near Auburn), the widely distributed report sparked many people to relocate here on a temporary or permanent basis.

Another beneficiary of the state report was Wilson's Inn opposite Napa Soda Springs. Wilson's was the perfect counterpoint to Colonel Jackson's opulent resort. This rustic retreat was founded by Arno and Ethel Brodt Wilson who boarded a modest forty or fifty guests in contrast to Napa Soda Springs' 250. All heating was done with wood stoves, and since the resort was never wired for electricity, lighting was by acetylene gas lamps. Tubercular patients were not accepted but all other noncontagious lung patients were welcome. A post office was established here in 1894, then discontinued in 1930 when many rural post offices were centralized in Napa. Wilson's was famous all over the country for its mountain grown apples shipped conveniently from its own post office. Several years after Wilson's was sold, Ethyl Brodt Wilson published a book of poems, *On a Blue Mountain*, about her experience living on Atlas Peak.

West of Foss Valley is the volcanic eminence called Stag's Leap. On its Napa Valley side a manor house made from hand-cut local stone was built by Horace Chase in the 1880s. His 200 acres of vineyard needed a home so a winery was constructed in 1893. For cellaring, caves were hand-dug to provide the perfect temperature and humidity. Stag's Leap was popular with San Francisco's elite. Two of their most famous visitors were the King and Queen of Portugal. The evocative Stag's Leap name is likely just a fancy moniker created by Horace Chase. The myth of the leaping stag who, cornered by hunters on one side and a deep chasm on the other, leapt the hundred foot gap to his freedom is probably even more fanciful. It is known, however, that deer were quite plentiful then as now, and gentlemen hunters were driven by coachmen to Napa Soda Springs to travel the distance back to Stag's Leap afoot in search of prey. Stag's Leap Winery was revived by Carl Doumani in the '60s

Hikers descend the Rector Ridge Trail

and '70s and is now one of the finest producers of wine in Napa Valley.

Rector Creek, draining Foss Valley from the north and emptying into the Napa River north of Yountville, is named for John P. Rector, a settler at the base of the canyon. Due to its rugged nature the canyon itself remained in a natural state until 1946. When the Veterans' Home of Yountville was established in 1884, their water supply was furnished by damming a small creek in the western hills creating Lake Hinman. Later, the state of California purchased lands in Rector Canyon as a water source for four state facilities, Napa State Hospital, the State Hospital Farm, the State Game Farm, and the Veterans' Home.

A 1926 Report on Water Supply for State Institutions

99

in Napa Valley recommended the water infrastructure be upgraded. It went on to note the excellent water yield of perennial Rector Creek and a potential dam site at the mouth of the canyon. Twenty years later on January 7, 1946, work began on Rector Dam. That summer an article in *Western Construction News* made this observation: "A 20-foot fault zone was discovered crossing the axis of the dam at about a 15 degree angle . . . however, the fault is believed to be well sealed by the grout curtain placed underneath . . . the dam." The fault they discovered was most likely inactive. Almost exactly one year after commencement, the earthfill dam was completed, impounding 4,400 acre feet of water at a cost of just over one million dollars.

Recently, management of some lands in this area were turned over to the California Department of Fish and Game which officially opened them to the public. Development of a hiking trail from Rector Ridge to Stag's Leap is anticipated as is its inclusion in the Bay Area Ridge Trail system.

TRAIL NOTES:

Find the unmarked trail's start at the southeast end of the Yountville Maintenance Facility which has expanded since the last edition of this book. Follow the fence line to the right until it ends, then start a steady, upward traverse to the east through grassy meadows of purple vetch, wild radish, and a super sized version of California poppy called frying pan poppy, with a smattering of blue oaks. You may see wild turkeys nesting. Cross a small streambed where poison oak and fiddlenecks (Amsinkia) grow, then pass under power lines. The rocky trail can be quite steep but in the spring is reliably softened by many wildflowers like sticky monkeyflower and Douglas lupine, a close relative of the bluebonnet, the Texas state flower. After crossing another gully where sage and sweet pea grow, the climb eases a bit as you round the shoulder of a hill.

Just below the ridge the trail splits, the left fork head-

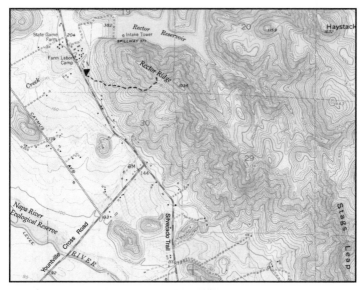

ing directly to the top and the right leading you along the ridge. When you reach the top you gain a great, perhaps surprising view of Rector Canyon, the serpentine lake behind the dam, and the compelling Haystack Peak which is prominent from many parts of the valley. East of the ridge is state owned land managed by the Department of Veteran Affairs. Here the developed trail ends. One day it will continue on to Stag's Leap. If you wish, turn southeast and wander along the ridge for a while avoiding the lush poison oak bushes which look like they were fertilized with Vigoro. In spring beautiful displays of bitterroot (Lewisia rediviva), the Montana state flower, bloom on several rocky outcrops. This ground hugging, succulent herb blooms in colors from white to pink or red to vibrant red-purple. The flowers have very large petals (2-3 inches) that nearly hide the fleshy leaves. Return the same way.

NAPA RIVER ECOLOGICAL RESERVE

The last significant stand of valley oaks in Napa Valley

DIRECTIONS: From Highway 29 at Yountville, go east on Madison for two blocks. Turn left on Yount, then right on Yountville Cross Road. After 1.1 miles, turn north before the bridge into an expanded parking lot for about ten cars. Vault toilets and a recycling bin are nearby. From Silverado Trail the turnoff is slightly less than a mile.

DISTANCE: 1¼-mile loop

GRADE: Easy. Minimal elevation gain or loss.

BEST TIME: Spring and fall

INFO: Dept. of Fish and Game, 707/944-5500

WARNING: The footbridge over the Napa River which led to the main trail was washed out and there are no plans to restore it. In winter or spring the river may be too difficult or dangerous to cross. You may want wading shoes for late spring through fall.

SUGGESTION: A short trail along the top of the levee follows the west bank.

In 1836 this property formed part of the southern boundary of George Yount's *Rancho Caymus*. Low-lying areas at the confluence of Conn Creek and Napa River would flood during many wet winters, often to a depth of three or four feet. By the turn of the century a levee was built on the west bank of Napa River to keep all but the highest floods out.

In 1851 began a tradition of church revivals lasting 28 years. They took place in the flat grassy area just beyond the present parking lot, known as the Yountville Camp Grounds. The Disciples of Christ denominational church, also known as Campbellites, held meetings here annually. Headed by local pastor Stormy John McCorkle, they were enormously popular affairs lasting a week or two, with as many as 4,000 people coming from all over the state. Some participants brought their own camping equipment, but those without had special accommodations built for them. Cooking facilities and long tables were set up to serve upwards of 1,000 meals a day. With the establishment of laundries, barber shops, a restaurant, and stores selling ice cream, candy, tobacco and cigars, the

Yountville Camp Grounds each year became a temporary small city.

The Methodist-Episcopal church and the Seventh Day Adventists also used this site. The tradition of outdoor camp meetings gave way after 1879 to indoor city conventions. Use of the Yountville Camp Grounds after that was limited to cattle grazing. It is unlikely the ground

103

was ever tilled for crops. The valley oak/bay laurel riparian forest on the eastern portion of the reserve is virtually unchanged since George Yount first drove his cattle through the river.

In 1974 threat of development prompted the Wildlife Conservation Board to buy this area to create the 73-acre Napa River Ecological Reserve. It was then turned over to California Department of Fish and Game for management. Farther up valley, one hundred acres of valley floor oak woodland between Bale Lane and Ehlers Lane met a sadder fate. Over seventy-five oaks up to 400 years old were destroyed by Beaucannon winery for vineyard in 1989. This was one of the finest parts of Napa Valley.

The importance of the Napa River Ecological Reserve cannot be overstated. It is the last significant stand of valley oak riparian woodland left in Napa Valley. Walking through here for the first time in December 1994, I was stunned to discover this beautiful piece had survived. It has the only stretch of the Napa River I've seen that looks inviting enough to swim. In 1994 the Napa Solano Audubon was awarded a grant of $7,300 to improve the overgrown CCC trail, and install a informational exhibit, benches, public toilet and for the printing of bird, animal and plant lists and a trail guide. Nearly 240 plant species live here, and 200 species of animals have been spotted including fox, deer, great horned owls, cedar waxwings, violet green swallows and the pipevine swallowtail butterfly.

TRAIL NOTES:

The trail heads north through the meadow once known as the Yountville Camp Grounds. Note that a live oak revegetation program has been started on both sides of the trail. Before the levee was built, the river plain may have been ½ mile wide here. Since the last edition, a four-board informational display has been installed. Unfortunately, some sun damage and graffiti has already occurred, but it is still well worth a look. Ascend to the levee top. Hundreds of sandbags were placed here during the floods of 1995, but could not prevent major damage to the levee. In June 1995 the levee was completely regraded and repaired.

As you head toward the river, vegetation on this old river terrace is dramatically different. The dominant overstory is valley and live oak with an understory of Santa Barbara sedge, Himalaya blackberry, and common snowberry. As you drop down to the river, vegetation undergoes another quick transformation to willows, smartweed and sedge.

The ecological reserve has long been misused by local partiers who leave trash of all descriptions. Lately the situation has deteriorated alarmingly, becoming not just an eyesore but unsanitary with cause for concern about illegal use of fire. Visitors are using the reserve as a public toilet. Barbecues and wood fires threaten the entire reserve and surrounding area. Most of the problem is confined to the riverbanks but has also spread into the main reserve. Fish and Game is underfunded and has no officer in charge of this site at press time. An agreement with the county to clean up the parking lot area is not sufficient. Of all the places in this book I've visited, the reserve is by far the greatest embarrassment. Visitors need to have more respect for this area and understand that many of their activities are not only illegal but damaging to the plant and animal community, and therefore ultimately to them. A volunteer citizens group to patrol, educate the public, and clean up the area is greatly needed.

At river level, follow it upstream briefly, then find a safe and shallow river crossing. You may see the wreckage of the old low water bridge which there are no plans to remove. Just south, Conn Creek joins the Napa River. Ascend the bank and pick up a trail guide at the start of the nature trail. If they're missing, contact Fish and Game or Napa Solano Audubon. Take the right fork to a fine meadow ringed by huge valley oaks, some five feet in diameter and eighty feet tall, and marvelous live oaks. Much of Napa Valley looked like this 150 years ago. As you begin the loop, some rare and/or endangered plants to look for among the reserve's 238 species are Sebastopol meadowfoam, Gairdner's yampah, pink star tulip and camas.

The trail now leads you along the west bank of Conn Creek, often dry in summer. Note the many young oak seedlings, sign of a healthy forest. You may hear the calls of acorn woodpecker, rufous-sided towhee, quail, and song sparrow here. Volunteers have installed bird boxes on the occasional oak tree. You will find a bench halfway along the loop. One quiet and unusually warm winter day I watched each gust of wind blow hundreds of dead and dying leaves from the trees to settle gently and peacefully in their final resting place. No one was around, making this a real oasis in the sea of busy-ness that Napa Valley has become.

The trail turns left to traverse the back of the preserve, then left again to follow the east bank of the Napa River past wild plum, bay laurel, and oaks. Watch for poison oak among the sedge and snowberry understory. With the right light, steelhead trout are easily seen in the river shadows. Across the river on the west bank some revetment and rock work has been done in an attempt to halt and/or reverse the effects of erosion on two great bay laurel trees.

The loop ends with a view of the great meadow at 1⅛ miles. You might return the trail guide to the holder for others to use. From here it is about ¼ mile to the parking lot.

ALSTON PARK

Napa City's second largest open space park

DIRECTIONS: From Highway 29 take Trower Avenue west. The southern park entrance is straight across Dry Creek Road. There is a second, north entrance .25 mile up Dry Creek Road.

DISTANCE: 2½-mile double loop

GRADE: Easy

BEST TIME: All year

DOG ALLOWED: On leash

INFO: Napa Community Resources Department, 707/257-9529

Chipped mortars and obsidian flakes found in a 1991 survey suggest Native Americans occupied this site sometime in the past. In historical times, the land has sustained heavy livestock grazing. The park primarily consists of non-native grass hills with some native purple needle grass (*Stipa pulchra*). A recent California Native Plant Society survey recorded a diversity of plant life, suggesting the area is slowly recovering.

In 1971 seventy-one acres in the southern portion of today's park, known as the Thomas property, were for sale. It was mostly prune orchard then, with some pears, cherries, peaches and walnuts. In 1978 the City of Napa purchased all of the present Alston Park and had plans for a community center and recreation facilities. Two years later the city council approved baseball and softball diamonds and lighting, soccer fields, tennis courts, a pool, picnic tables, trails and a community hall. That's when, you might say, the prunes hit the orchard fan.

Disapproval of the idea erupted city wide. Wine growers were appalled that prime viticulture land would be paved over. Taxpayers refused to foot the maintenance bill. One group, the Citizens for Alston Alternatives, took out full page ads in the newspaper to ask pointed questions. Why sink $10 million into another recreation complex when neglected Kennedy Park was already there? The proposal was defeated in 1981.

Ten years later in 1991 Alston Park opened as a passive use open space park. It offers something for almost everyone — walkers, joggers, mountain bikers, equestrians and dog owners, who have formed their own support group — ADOG (Alston Dog Owners Group). The City of Napa owns it and its Community Resources Department maintains it. Users will find restrooms, water, and three picnic sites available in the 157-acre park. Eight well maintained trails provide three miles of walking. Trail maps are found at Napa Community Resources Department, 1100 West Street near the Cine Dome Theatre in Napa.

TRAIL NOTES:

The following two loop trails allow you to see the entire park.
LOOP 1 (2 miles)

Take Valley View Trail to Orchard Trail past naturalized fruit trees. On the way are wooden bridges crossing two small creeks that flow in winter. Past the north entrance continue on Dry Creek Trail. On the north side of the park is a major oak replanting project, young trees protected by plastic tubes. Stands of live oak, valley oak, and madrone on Dry Creek make excellent natural picnic sites in spring.

From the west hilltop, in the forested slopes above Redwood Creek, the henna-colored trunks of redwood stand out against the darker evergreens. Here, a dead-end side trail leads to the best part of the park. Don't miss it. It leads downhill past oaks draped with Spanish moss. In the flat

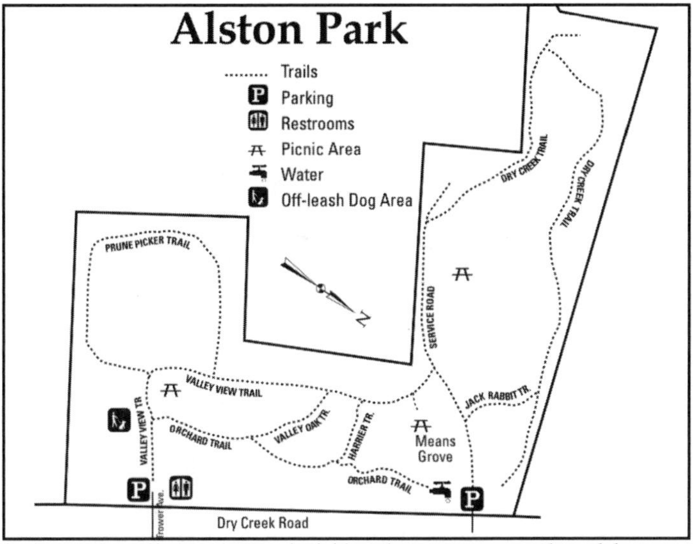
Alston Park
Trails
Parking
Restrooms
Picnic Area
Water
Off-leash Dog Area
PRUNE PICKER TRAIL
N
SERVICE ROAD
DRY CREEK TRAIL
DRY CREEK TRAIL
VALLEY VIEW TRAIL
VALLEY VIEW TR.
ORCHARD TRAIL
VALLEY OAK TR.
HARRIER TR.
JACK RABBIT TR.
Means
Grove
ORCHARD TRAIL
Trower Ave.
Dry Creek Road

below are valley oaks and old buckeye trees, with wild grape in Redwood Creek, a cool place to head for in summer.

Back on Dry Creek Trail turn east and parallel an extensive vineyard that separates the north and south portions of the park. Just before joining the service road you pass the Pacifica Water Tank, built in 1960 in response to the exploding housing development in Brown's Valley. Join Valley View Trail. Immediately a connector trail leads to a picnic site and Means (Memorial) Grove. Continue past two more trail junctions to Prune Picker Trail.

To the left is a giant wreck of a valley oak. One morning I saw a kestrel fly to the top of it with a meal. Chunks of fur went flying every time he took a bite. The black-tipped red tail of the falcon was split, with the bottom half constantly bobbing up and down. Alston is a good place to see these beautiful raptors.

LOOP 2 (½ mile)

The Prune Picker Trail takes off from Valley View Trail and ends on the same trail, taking a loop around an abandoned orchard. It's a suitable length for a morning walk before work. It can be accessed also by a narrow entrance in the southeast corner of the park.

WESTWOOD HILLS REGIONAL PARK

Oak woodland countryside within Napa city limits

DIRECTIONS: From Highway 29 in Napa take First Street exit west, then continue as it becomes Brown's Valley Road. After 1 mile the park entrance is on your left.

DISTANCE: 2-mile loop

GRADE: Easy

BEST TIME: All year

INFO: Napa Community Resources Department, 707/257-9529

FACILITIES: Picnic tables, water fountain

SUGGESTIONS: Trail maps are available from the Carolyn Parr Nature Museum found on the west border of the park. It's open weekends during the school year from 1–4 p.m. and in summer Tuesday–Sunday 1–4 p.m. The museum has exhibits and dioramas depicting the plants, animals and geology of Napa County, plus children's and adult nature libraries. Volunteers needed. 707/255 6465

Napa County Land Trust's Connally Ranch is at the corner of Brown's Valley Road and Thompson Avenue. Tours are by appointment only. For information call 707/252-3270.

Threat of housing development in the 1970s almost consigned Westwood Hills to history. In 1974 a developer proposed building 350 homes on this beautiful 110-acre parcel. The scaled-down version counter-offered by the city did not interest the developer. That's when the city proposed to buy the parcel for parkland.

For many years Westwood Hills was used for grazing cattle. When the old rancher died his heirs wished to sell. They liked the idea of saving the land as a park, and waited until sufficient money was appropriated. The City of Napa bought the land in 1975 for $160,000, about $1,500 an acre. The man who spearheaded this effort was former Napa City Planner Mike Joell. The park opened in January 1976.

Literally thousands of hours of volunteer time went into building trails, installing benches and tables, and readying the park for opening. California Conservation Corps built many of the trails, the National Guard worked on some roads and today local environmental groups and the Boy Scouts still do maintenance and improvements.

Drought conditions in 1976 invited a grass fire to race through that first summer. Rocky Ridge Trail was created in a futile attempt to block the fire's progress. Eucalyptus on that ridge and in Gum Canyon were destroyed along with some live oaks. It is worth noting that deer-browsed trees were saved while those with branches touching the ground caught fire.

New policies were set as a result. Because controlled burns were unsafe so close to urban areas, it was decided that 1) fuel sources like eucalyptus and Scotch broom should be eliminated, 2) all important trees should be kept trimmed above ground, 3) cattle would graze here May to October to moderate fuel sources, and 4) buffer zones around the park were necessary for public safety. Today, the persnickety eucalyptus cut to the ground after the fire have regrown, showing that element of the solution needs rethinking.

In 1980 the property just south of Hilltop was bought cheaply at auction by developer Leroy Young. Soon after, an exemption was granted to allow a water hookup. Despite vociferous public outcry, a large three-story house that includes a two-story racquet ball court was built. Still under construction, the house has never been occupied. After a neighbor filed a lawsuit, approximately thirty city code violations were discovered, including a lack of permits for transmission tower installation. A second exemption was sought for another house but denied. In the face of community opposition, individualist Young has shown his sense of humor by erecting a smiley face made of pvc pipe and lit by Christmas lights, visible at night all over the city.

Westwood Hills today enjoys great popularity throughout the year. There are no immediate plans for expansion, but one day it may be connected to the Connally Ranch by trail. Also on the wish list is a permanent home for the Carolyn Parr Museum.

TRAIL NOTES:

Westwood Hills is small enough (110 acres) that you'll be able to see it all in an hour's brisk walk. The described trail mainly uses the smaller trails and avoids all but short sections of roadway. Of course any combination of trails or roads may be taken.

Take the road, Valley View Trail, from the parking lot past a locked gate. The old farmhouse on your left is the original dwelling of the rancher who grazed cattle on this property. Young eucalyptus groves appear first on the right then on both sides. The fire of July 1976 killed most of these trees, some 200 feet tall. Almost everything here is regrowth. As you pass by a second gate, a water trough to the left is one used by cattle that graze park hills in the summer months. Vegetation turns native with bay and live oak overstory.

Immediately after a tall Monterey cypress and a resting bench, turn right on an unnamed trail at ¼ mile. Soon you pass a third gate. This section of trail was built by a young man in a wheelchair. Just below the top of the knoll the trail appears to veer right, but it soon leads onto private property. Turn left and continue up through oak, bay and madrone woodlands with lots of poison oak underfoot.

Come to a trail junction at ⅜ mile. Turn left briefly onto Rocky Ridge Trail and pass a fourth gate. Soon take the first unmarked right turn onto the Red Hawk Trail. At another signed trail junction stay right and head downhill. A stone wall plunges toward Thompson Street. Hand-built walls like these were made between 100 and 150 years ago, both to clear fields of rocks and serve as property boundaries. At ½ mile descend wooden steps placed by inmates (they do much trail and fire work in the county). Watch for wildflowers in spring at an open meadow. In winter this hillside is running with water and slippery. Near the park's west boundary a trail leads to one of the two entrances on Thompson Avenue.

A concrete-pipe bridge at ⅝ mile crosses a small creek. To the left a live oak has sent a limb snaking along the ground for forty feet in search of sun. You soon arrive at

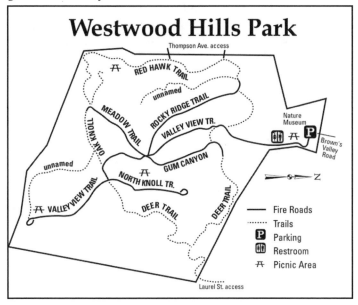

Westwood Hills Park

Thompson Ave. access

RED HAWK TRAIL

unnamed

ROCKY RIDGE TRAIL

MEADOW TRAIL

OAK KNOLL

VALLEY VIEW TR.

Nature Museum

Brown's Valley Road

unnamed

GUM CANYON

NORTH KNOLL TR.

VALLEY VIEW TRAIL

DEER TRAIL

DEER TRAIL

—— Fire Roads
········· Trails
🅿 Parking
🚻 Restroom
🏕 Picnic Area

Laurel St. access

the other Thompson Avenue entrance. This was once the only entrance to the park. You will see what looks like the remains of a stone cistern. After a short climb, traverse a grassy hill veering first south then east.

The Red Hawk Trail ends beyond ¾ mile. To the left is Oak Knoll, with a picnic table under graceful oaks. At one time the ten acres around it was the only land proposed as a park. Turn right onto Oak Knoll Trail through the finest oak woodland in the park. Soon come to a signed trail junction. Oak Knoll goes left. Stay right on an unnamed trail and go steeply uphill to a meadow. The narrow, stony trail ahead was cut by volunteers with hand chisels. Use caution here in winter when it's wet.

At mile 1 turn left up wooden steps at the fence boundary. On your left is an awesome live oak estimated at 300 years old. Three of its huge limbs have sagged to the ground for some distance. Cows like it under here. For some reason, their altar-shaped cow patty piles have a vague ceremonial look about them. The trail rises steeply to the ridgetop past a tree restoration project.

Soon you reach Hilltop, high point of the park. This used to be a 360 degree view, but a mansion now blocks the sight

114

of San Francisco and the Golden Gate Bridge. Although the Spanish tile roof and whitewashed walls would be attractive in a neighborhood, it is an out-of-place eyesore in this location. That goes double for the communications towers.

Still visible are three landmarks of the Bay Area — Mount St. Helena, Mount Tamalpais and Mount Diablo. Almost the whole town of Napa is laid out below. Down the hill east might be seen cattle of the owner who has grazing rights to the park. A bench and table are provided for rest and/or picnicking.

Now back on Valley View Trail, walk along the level top, then drop to a three-trail junction beyond 1¼ miles where a graffitti-scrawled picnic table and trash can are chained to a dying madrone. Take the right fork, walking on narrow Deer Trail under an arched tree branch. Soon Mount George (1,877 feet) looms due east. The steep hillside trail takes you past a draw with a buckeye grove.

Begin the steep descent near an oak stump, passing bare hillside to an unmarked trail junction. To the right a trail leads to a fourth park entrance/exit at Laurel Street. Continue straight and come to so-called Cardboard Hill, a dirt hillside on the right where kids used to ride homemade sleds. Re-enter an oak forest where a barbed wire fence is close enough to tear your clothes.

A trail junction with Gum Canyon Trail is at 1¾ miles. Stay right on Deer Trail, head slightly uphill and then left at an arrowed sign. The remains of a stone pond used to water cattle marks this area. Soon you arrive at the junction with Valley View Trail. Turn right and go ¼ mile to the parking lot for a total distance of just over 2 miles.

NAPA RIVER TRAIL

River front access along an old historic waterway

Nathan Coombs chose the site for the city of Napa for one reason — it was as far upriver as large boats could navigate. The burgeoning river commerce that Coombs foresaw fostered Napa for half a century. The river then sustained another fifty years of neglect and abuse. As we enter the new millennium, long range plans for the river's renewal and care are coming to fruition. The City of Napa's Napa River and Napa Creek Flood Protection Project broke ground in August 2000. It is a model of interagency cooperation that cities all over the world are watching. It should make Napans proud again of their historic waterway.

Native Americans lived along the river for thousands of years, using boats made of tule reeds to fish and to cross from one bank to the other. Two tribes, the Wappo and Patwin, both lived in the vicinity of present day Napa. The tribal boundary line was roughly the confluence of Napa Creek and Napa River, with the Wappo north of there, the Patwin south.

Indians were still very much a presence in 1836 when Nicolas Higuera was granted *Rancho Entre Napa* by Mexico. It included that land which is now the city of Napa and the Carneros to the west. Nathan Coombs was only twenty-two when he received land along the river in exchange for building a barn for Higuera. Coombs founded Napa in 1848 — the same year James Marshall found gold in Coloma.

Often men who failed to find gold in the Sierra struck

it rich in Napa. They bought cheap valley land and raised crops from deep, virgin, volcanic soil. They raised cattle for hides and tallow — Napa's first industry — or grew wheat and fruit. As San Francisco blossomed, Napa farmers and ranchers supplied the city with its bounty. No all-year roads existed, no bridges over the river. There was only one highway in those days — the river.

Located where the river was navigable at low tide, the town of Suscol, founded by Mariano Vallejo, was competitive with Napa for a short time. The first ferry operated there by 1852, connecting the Sacramento–Petaluma overland stage route. Steamships would bring visitors and tourists from San Francisco who disembarked at Suscol to take stage and later rail service to up-valley resorts.

Heavy industry, though, favored Napa. Tanneries, lumber yards, gas works and warehouses full of grain, apple orchards and vineyards lined the river front for miles. As many as seven different wharves operated at one time. The work horse of the river was the scow schooner, built to carry heavy loads and move quickly, rarely drafting more than twenty-two inches of water. These boats took local agricultural goods, oats, wheat, corn, puncheons of wine and hides, to San Francisco and returned with finished products, machinery, tools, and sewer pipes.

Lumber schooners designed to sail the open sea brought in lumber from Mendocino mills and left with tan bark from the forests of Mount St. Helena. As many as fifty ships a day jostled for space on the Napa River.

Napa prospered. Wealthy merchants and river captains built Victorian mansions which still stand near Division Street. They simply walked out their front door to work. The river-driven economy lasted until Henry Ford's invention, when roads and bridges made access to Napa easy. The era closed when the steamship *Zinfandel* made its last run in 1920.

Abuse of the waterway followed neglect. The river served as an unofficial trash dump, while sewer lines emptied directly into the river. Amazingly, the only other water source for Napa until 1924, besides backyard wells, was the Napa River itself. A small dam backed up a quarter mile-long lake just upstream from the Trancas Bridge. Water was filtered through an old locomotive boiler filled with sand. Poor water quality, brackish and black with manganese and iron, plus lack of water pressure in the mains, brought the swift completion of Milliken Dam in the eastern hills.

Mare Island Naval Base revitalized a slumping Napa economy by 1941, doubling then redoubling the population. Increasing abuse of the river wasn't addressed until 1948 when Napa Sanitation District was formed. Many residents remember the river so toxic it would kill fish by the thousands and peel paint off nearby buildings. By 1953, storm and sewer lines were separated and the river began to heal.

Out of a flood control proposal in the early 1960s has grown a multipurpose environmental project, the Napa River and Napa Creek Flood Protection Project. A strong community coalition along with a phalanx of federal, state and local agencies are involved. They have replaced the old concept of controlling nature through channelization with the idea of allowing the river the space it needs in wet winters. Flood control will be accomplished by higher clearance bridges in downtown Napa, channel widening to create more natural flood terraces, dike lowering or removal, and wetland, riparian and upland restoration. New dikes, levees and floodwalls at higher elevations will contain a 100-year flood event. Fishers will have improved access with six new piers. Hikers and bicyclists will have five miles of trail on the west bank of the river and one mile on the east bank to enjoy, from John F. Kennedy Park on the south end to Trancas Street on the north. Parks and Recreation has plans to connect the river trail with other regional trails like the Bay Area Ridge Trail, the Bay Trail, and Napa Valley Trail (along the river to Calistoga).

A new respect is emerging for our waterways and wetlands. Although only one eighth of Napa County's original wetlands remain, conservationists are striving to save what's left. Recently 9,850 acres of the Napa Marsh were purchased through

Proposition 117 funds. The marshes are important wintering habitat for twenty-five species of Pacific flyway waterfowl. Twelve thousand canvasbacks have been seen at a time.

The Napa River, despite a listing of impaired status by the EPA, remains one of the best steelhead streams in the Bay Area, with spawning on Redwood, Brown's Valley, Milliken, Tulocay and Napa creeks. The rare Mason's quillwort (*Lilaeopsis masonii*) may be found on old pilings in the Napa River and along Old Tulocay Creek. In recent years, a sea lion, a gray whale and a river otter have been seen frolicking in these waters. With understanding of its past and care for its future, the Napa River may emerge from its tarnished image to reclaim a place in Napans' hearts.

TRANCAS to LINCOLN

DIRECTIONS:	From Highway 29 in Napa drive east on Trancas Street 1.5 miles, or .5 mile from the Silverado Trail. Look for the hiker access sign on the west side of the Napa River.
DISTANCE:	1¼ miles one way
GRADE:	Easy, mostly level walking.
BEST TIME:	All year
DOGS ALLOWED:	On leash
INFO:	Napa Community Resources Department, 707/257-9529

TRAIL NOTES:

Here on this segment one can see most clearly what a wonderful concept the Napa River Trail is, and when finished what a huge asset it will be to the city. Since the second edition of this guide, the trail here has gone from a rough trail with little traffic to a multiuse paved path popular with walkers, joggers, bicyclists, dog owners, fishers and inline skaters.

Your path starts on the south side of busy Trancas Street (in the future, the trail will have a dedicated parking lot on the north side of Trancas with a tunnel under the street) and runs between the Napa River on the east and housing tracts to the west. The riverbank grows wild with native and introduced species — blackberry, ivy, periwinkle and wild grape under live oak and bay. Bird life is abundant along the river. In the bushes look for robins, jays, finches, quail and juncos while in the tree tops you might spot owls, red-tailed hawks, crows and vultures. Social trails lead to the river.

You'll find three access points off Soscol Avenue between here and Lincoln: at Towpath Village at ¼ mile, at Elks Way at ⅓ mile, and at ⅝ mile, stairs leading to Shoreline Drive. Most of the trail has a neat and attractive appearance now with resting benches facing the river and even trash cans provided along the way. After a mile the pavement ends and turns to gravel near where flood damage eroded the riverbank in 2006. Repairs are planned and in the funding stage. You'll start to see a series of small, attractive, blue, red and brown housing units. This is the new River Pointe resort billed as California Vacation Cottages. The trail ends at Lincoln Avenue. Completion of the trail is now scheduled for 2013 in conjunction with the entire Napa River Flood Control Project.

KENNEDY PARK to IMOLA

DIRECTIONS:	From Highway 29 take Imola Avenue east to Soscol Avenue. Turn right. Just past Napa Valley College turn right again on Streblow Drive. Follow it past the golf course, over the railroad tracks, then follow the River Trail signs to the boat launch area.
DISTANCE:	1¼ mile one way
HOURS:	7 a.m. to 9 p.m.
GRADE:	Easy, all level walking
BEST TIME:	Winter for birding, all year for walking
DOGS ALLOWED:	On leash
INFO:	Napa Community Resources Department, 707/257-9529

120

SUGGESTIONS: Wheelchair accessible. Bring binoculars for viewing bird life. Additional trails in the area can be found at Stanley Lane near the junction of Highway 29 and Highway 12/121, leading to the river at Cuttings Wharf.

TRAIL NOTES:

From the boat launch, find a display case to the right which marks the trail's start. A map shows present and future trail development. The six-mile long trail has four segments: Kennedy Park, Napa Abajo (the old light industry area), downtown waterfront, and the Woodlands (Lincoln to Trancas). The trail is a wide, blacktop pavement accommodating walkers, bicyclists and dogs on leash. This walk will become increasingly popular due to its accessibility, easy level grade and safety.

The trail does some pleasant meanderings past Kennedy Park's picnic grounds and ball fields. Between the trail and the river is an extensive border planting of native plants like cottonwood, oak, alder and coyote brush, a project of the Army Corps of Engineers as part of the Napa River Flood Control Project. At ⅓ mile a parallel dirt track winds through a new grove of sycamore trees. To the right are solar panels producing energy for Napa Valley College. Out here in the open spaces you may see the black-shouldered kites hovering in midair in search of prey.

The trail now runs straight for nearly ½ mile until crossing a footbridge over an abandoned cutoff of Tulocay Creek. To the left is the Marina, where it seems every house has a dock and a boat out front. Soon you cross under the new bridge that replaced the old but pictur-esque Maxwell drawbridge. This new one has some striking architectural lines similar to the Southern Crossing seen to the south. The pavement ends and so does the trail, at press time, at 1¼ miles.

KENNEDY PARK LOOP

DISTANCE: ¾ mile
GRADE: Easy
OPEN: Sunrise to Sunset
DOGS ALLOWED: On leash
WARNING: Heads up for remote controlled model air-
                    planes flying overhead.

TRAIL NOTES:

The trail's start is to the left of the boat launch. The old rutted dirt track has been replaced by wide blacktop pavement. Access to the river is close by for the first ¼ mile with informal trails that lead to the river where fishers ply their lines for sturgeon, striped bass, flounder and mudsuckers. Sturgeon is an ancient species capable of living two to three hundred years and weighing 1800 pounds. Legal limit size however is between four and six feet and around a hundred pounds.

On the left is a circular paved area where model plane hobbyists fly radio-controlled craft or larger models on a tether. Across the river to the west is a permanent wildlife refuge known as the Stewart Ranch. The banks of the river hold a mix of non-native trees like acacia and pine. The trail veers left around new baseball fields with views across the slough to the southeast of Napa's steel and pipe works.

On the return leg you pass the BMX grounds and four tall transmitter towers belonging to radio station KVON. The sunken circular area they stand in was formerly used as settling ponds for Napa River dredge spoils. End the loop at ¾ mile. This walk will only become more popular with all kinds of people including joggers, moms with baby strollers, and those needing exercise on their lunch breaks.

RIVER TO RIDGE TRAIL

Connector trail between Kennedy Park and Skyline Wilderness Park

DIRECTIONS: From Highway 29 take Imola Avenue east to Soscol Avenue. Turn right on Soscol. Just past Napa Valley College turn right again on Streblow Avenue. Go 0.2 mile and turn left into the parking lot for the Formal Garden.

HOURS: Monday-Friday 9-5, Saturday-Sunday 8-5

FEES: $3 for hikers, $4 for horses and bicycles, on the honor system

DISTANCE: 1½ miles one way

GRADE: Easy

BEST TIME: Spring, winter

DOGS: On leash

INFO: Skyline Wilderness Park, 707/252-0481

WARNING: Gate is locked at 5 p.m.

TRAIL NOTES:

River to Ridge Trail, a part of both the Bay Trail system and the Bay Area Ridge Trail system, begins as an easement between Napa State Hospital and Syar properties. River to Ridge starts on the east side of the intersection of Highway 221 and Streblow Avenue. The easement begins in a narrow corridor with tall fencing on either side. It borders a small creek on the right with live oak overstory, and an understory of poison oak and Himalayan blackberry. Note one lone escapee camphor tree in the mix. At ⅓ mile the trail opens up into oak grasslands. During the week you may here a background roar of industrial noise to the south.

It appears the trail is a popular destination due to the college being so near. Although it is showing some signs of wear, it is generally in good shape. Beyond ⅜ mile begin a slight uphill climb. Beyond ½ mile industrial noise will abate. Take a sharp left, climb a bit and soon a bridge to bridge view (Imola to the Southern Crossing) of lower Napa appears with some of the bigger regional mountains in the background like Mount Tamalpais and Mount Veeder.

At one mile you'll find a convenient, natural sitting rock. Go through an old, ungated fence and pass a small obvious cutout in the hillside, perhaps an old quarry or spring. The forest spruces up a bit with black oaks. At 1¼ miles you'll notice a massive water tank which supplies the city of Napa. Follow the trail arrow left and down through more open buckeye groves, which soon afford views of Mount George and Skyline Park. Cross the access road to the water tank and follow another arrow sign straight ahead. Before 1½ miles is a curious remnant of another age. A concrete retaining wall about twenty feet high has three openings each with a metal spout filling with leaf debris. This is a remnant from the Napa State Asylum days, perhaps a grain loader. To the left is dry Lake Como, once fed by springs that have disappeared. Beyond 1½ miles you meet the Skyline Trail. Return the same way or continue on into the park.

Along the Napa River Trail

SKYLINE WILDERNESS PARK

Old state hospital grounds offer the most hiking in the south county

DIRECTIONS: In the city of Napa, from Highway 221 or Highway 29, take Imola Avenue east to its end at Fourth Avenue.

HOURS: Monday-Thursday 9 a.m. to dark, Friday-Sunday 8 a.m. to dark

FEE: $5 per vehicle for hikers, $6/vehicle for equestrians and cyclists. Camping: $25-27/night for RV's. $8/night for tents

BEST TIME: Spring

INFO: Skyline Park, 707/252-0481

In October 1841, Cayetano Juarez received the Mexican Land Grant he called *Rancho Tulocay*. Located east of the present city of Napa, it included the land where Napa Valley College, Kennedy Park and Napa State Hospital are today. The Old Adobe Hut is part of the original Juarez home and still stands on Soscol Avenue. Juarez sold a portion of his ranch to the State of California in 1873.

When the Napa Asylum for the Insane arose in 1875, it was the most impressive building in the state. The Gothic Farmhouse was said to be a mile in circumference, made of slate, marble and nine million bricks made on site. It was five stories high, decorated with gargoyles and crowned

125

with seven towers, the highest 175 feet tall. Called domestic Gothic by its architect, later generations perceived it as scary European medieval. The causes of insanity were not well understood then. Patients were admitted for such reasons as business problems, religion and trouble in love.

Funds for maintenance were limited, so a mammoth agricultural operation was instigated to help defray costs. The 500 patients raised vegetable crops, worked the orchards and vineyards, and tended dairy herds and pigs. Some patients were admitted for marginal reasons and cured readily. Some of these were poor, without homes or families, and once released had nowhere to go. Thus began the tradition of former patients living in the woods of present Skyline Park.

Between 1876 and 1881 land behind the hospital was bought from William Coombs, brother of Napa's founder Nathan Coombs. The first structure built by the hospital in 1873, the small Coombs Ranch Dam, was no longer supplying sufficient water for the growing hospital. In the next ten years, Lake Louise, Lake Camille, and Lake Como were built for both practical and aesthetic reasons. The final property purchases in 1906 and 1908 took the hospital lands to the Solano County line. They were bought expressly to build

Water exploration cave

another reservoir, Lake Marie. This was finished in two stages for $91,000 and became the main water supply.

Before World War II a popular pastime with automobile owners was to take a drive through the grounds for picnicking and swimming. The hospital had its own post office, and mail was often addressed to Imola, California. The name appears to come from Italy, the center of that country's mental institutions.

Social and economic forces that changed so many things after World War II also came to Napa State Hospital. Local business groups complained that farm therapy, in which patients worked the land for free, was unfair competition. Treatment of patients had changed radically, modern drug therapy bringing care indoors. Also the hospital, not intended for use day and night, was badly overcrowded. In 1949 it was declared unfit for human habitation and torn down after seventy-six years of service. Demolition was mostly by wrecking ball, except for the rock-solid main tower which the workmen had to destroy by dynamite.

In 1969 the State of California had no more use for the wild lands behind the hospital and announced intentions to sell to private buyers. Environmentalists had a better idea and begged the county for a park. The county refused, but a novel idea emerged. By 1978 the Skyline Park Citizens Committee was leasing the land from the county, who in turn had a lease from the state, a unique solution.

The 850-acre park opened in February 1980. With minimal government funding, Skyline Park Citizens Association has run the park on a shoestring budget raised by user fees, fundraisers and private donations, all on volunteer effort. Near the entrance are a campground, an archery range, a community hall, and the continually growing Martha Walker Native Plant Garden. The Napa/Solano chapter of the California Native Plant Society holds spring and fall plant sales here.

The park today features over 17 miles of hiking on twelve trails, from old-growth oak woodland on hilltops to sunny meadows full of wildflowers in spring, to cool streamside pleasure under bay and alder canopy. Wildlife includes deer, coyote, large flocks of wild turkey, wild pig and birds of prey.

LAKE MARIE ROAD

Skyline's most popular trail

DISTANCE: 2 miles one way (add ⅜ mile to get to trail-head from entrance)

GRADE: Easy

ELEVATION GAIN: 650 feet

TRAIL NOTES:

From the parking lot's south corner take the signed trail, then turn to the right before the native plant garden. Take the grassy path west to a road and turn left. Follow the fenced corridor between Lake Camille and Lake Louise. The odd structure on your left, looking like a stone crypt, was once the pumping plant for now dry Lake Como to your right. You soon arrive at a trail junction, with Buckeye and Skyline trails starting a short distance up the trail to your right.

Take the left fork onto Lake Marie Road, following the rocky and rutted road you may share with horses and bike riders. On your left is Camp Coombs, still part of Napa State Hospital. These fruit and nut trees — peach, fig, olive and walnut — were once tended by hospital patients. Great masses of striped white eyes and seepspring monkeyflowers grow on the thin-soil hillsides in spring.

The road climbs steeply to a trail junction with a piped-spring horse trough at ¼ mile. The adventuresome Lower Marie Creek Trail starts here. Also at this junction is the Oakleaf Trail, which climbs the hill briefly then parallels Lake Marie Road for ½ mile before joining again. Continue straight past a shallow, fern-rimmed cave that most likely was dug for water exploration.

The steep climb proffers a bench for the weary at ½ mile, then a view of striking cliff formations in Marie Creek. These are known locally as Little Yosemite. Top the hill at ⅝ mile. The red wooden structure up the hill to your right is a wildlife viewing platform built by the Boy Scouts. A lengthy

128

stone wall descends from it and in broken fashion crosses the creek and climbs the eastern hillside. Although no one knows for certain, it may be stonework from the nineteenth century to mark property boundaries. These are found in many parts of the park.

Descending, you pass the Oakleaf Trail junction and leave the city noise of Napa behind. The Bayleaf Trail joins at ⅞

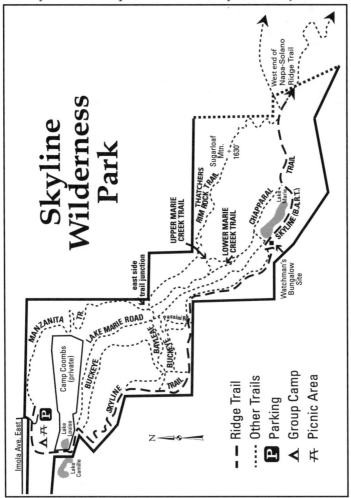

Skyline Wilderness Park

Ridge Trail
Other Trails
Parking
Group Camp
Picnic Area

Fig Tree Meadow on Lake Marie Road

mile and across from here is the enormous, venerable Fig Tree. This edible fig creates its own microclimate with a ground-to-ground canopy. It's probably one hundred years old.

Just uphill is the best picnic site in the park. A table under a big oak overlooks a meadow with at least one Indian grinding rock. A cute outhouse with a star and crescent moon design above the door can be found in the little meadow behind the table. Through the meadow and across the creek are Manzanita, Rim Rock and Marie Creek trails. Continue on Lake Marie Road past the Passini Road junction at mile 1. Stone wall remnants abound here. Descend into shadier oak/bay woodland.

A cave just beyond has a charming waterfall in the winter. The cave goes back at least twenty feet, with standing water on the cave floor. The vegetation becomes lush at 1¼ miles. Down in the creek are alder trees up to one hundred feet tall. The next ¼ mile holds the strangest and most mysterious sights in Skyline. Weird ruins reminiscent of ancient Egypt, or Mayan temples moldering in tropical jungles come to mind. Historians still haven't found the answers to their origin.

Down in Marie Creek is the only redwood in the upper park. It was introduced, since redwoods don't occur here naturally. The forest is dense with oak, madrone and soaring columns of bay laurel. At 1⅞ miles an unmarked road leads left to a meadow and picnic table at the base of the earthen dam. (No need to conjure images of the San Francisquito dam disaster of 1925 while eating lunch here. The dam is considered safe and as an extra precaution the lake level was lowered permanently after 1986.) Immediately beyond are two connectors with Skyline Trail, one signed.

Reach Lake Marie, your destination, at mile 2. There is a crossbar to tie your horse to, a bench and a trash can, I guess for those whose empty lunch sacks are too heavy to carry out. Swimming isn't allowed here but the bass fishing is said to be excellent.

THATCHER'S RIM ROCK TRAIL

Best views in the park

DISTANCE: 2¾ miles one way (to get to this trailhead, add 1 mile via Lake Marie Road, 1⅝ miles using Manzanita Trail)
GRADE: Moderate
ELEVATION GAIN: 1,500 feet

TRAIL NOTES:

At the four-way junction find the Rim Rock Trail sign directing you uphill. Go through a gap in a stone wall, then turn right before the chain link fence. Ascend gradually through manzanita and oak. The trail mostly avoids a thicket of chamise, and rewards you with a view into beautiful Marie Canyon after ¼ mile.

The trail starts to climb steeply and as you approach the ½-mile mark, Mount Veeder appears to the west, and beyond it, parts of Sonoma County. As you leave oak woodland, red volcanic rock outcroppings rise above the trail. From here, Mount Cobb to the northwest in Lake County is seen juxtaposed with Mount St. Helena.

At ¾ mile you skirt the headwaters of a very small canyon with fine old coast live oak overhead. A series of steep switchbacks begin and soon you are high enough to see Mount Tamalpais in Marin County. In late afternoon, sunlight glinting golden off the rivers, bays and estuaries give the serpentine complex of San Pablo Bay a rare beauty.

At 1¼ miles after passing a classic oak and grass hilltop, emerge from the woodland, contouring up and left through a meadow to the property fenceline by a huge oak. Take a series of switchbacks now while enjoying stupendous views of San Francisco Bay and Mount Tamalpais. Once you reach the ridgeline around 1½ miles, you'll have the best views in the park. All of Napa Valley from the foot of Mount St. Helena to the San Pablo Bay is visible. You can trace fifty miles of the Napa River from its source to its end at Mare Island Strait. Bring your panorama camera for this one. On a crystal clear day San Francisco and the Golden Gate Bridge look within paraglider range.

Near the top the trail levels out for easier walking. Before 1¾ miles you'll see a hilltop microwave station to the northeast. This is East Sugarloaf (1,686 feet). Come to the rounded, anti-climactic top of West Sugarloaf (1,630 feet), then coast downhill through oak/bay forest. A few hundred feet of the trail were steep and loose at press time. To the south you have a wonderful new perspective on upper Skyline Park, with Mount Diablo and the oil refinery on Highway 80 beyond. With the mountainside blocking all sounds of the city, it can be very peaceful here. In spring you'll see seepspring monkeyflower, lupine and fiddlenecks watered by a hillside seep.

Round a bluff for views again of Mount Tam, contouring through an open meadow past coyote brush, sage, poppies and numerous rock outcrops. Drop steeply on short, often rocky switchbacks. Closer to the stream buckeyes and oaks reappear as you soon arrive at the junction with Skyline Trail at 2½ miles. From here you can take a short jog to the east boundary and/or take Skyline Trail back for perhaps the park's ultimate loop trip.

SKYLINE TRAIL

The first dedicated section of Bay Area Ridge Trail in the North Bay

DISTANCE: 3½ miles one way (from the parking lot it is 8+ miles round trip)

GRADE: Strenuous

ELEVATION GAIN: 1,000 feet

TRAIL NOTES:

After the ⅜-mile approach, turn right at the trailhead junction. To the right is dry Lake Como, created by an earthen levee in 1890. It was once fed by springs that have vanished. The open maw of the quarry looms to the south. It was originally a state hospital operation but has been leased to Basalt Rock for many years.

Beyond ⅛ mile pass by the bike and horse alternate trail and come to the Skyline turnoff. Turn left and immediately the trail narrows and climbs steeply. The well constructed trail ascends a rocky meadow in sweeping curves. On the fringes are groves of buckeye, oak and bay. Many seeps and springs water a colorful variety of native wildflowers in spring. Displays of striped white eyes (related to baby blue eyes) are especially amazing, some years numbering in the hundreds of thousands. In winter the quarry becomes a lake.

Starting at ½ mile, each westerly bend of the trail contacts a stone wall, built in the nineteenth century ranching days. This is the longest stone wall in the park, one which you will see for two miles. Go through an opening in a redwood stake fence and look on the left for a grand old oak 200 to 300 years old.

Leave the oak grassland behind at ¾ mile and enter mixed evergreen forest. Trailside poison oak is rank. The steepest part of the Skyline Trail soon ends after climbing 600 vertical feet. At the stone wall the trail makes a right angle turn southeast. There is a fine grassy picnic area under oak and bay but watch for poison oak. Beyond the wall are views of the Napa Marsh and Mount Tamalpais. Pass by the Bayleaf Trail junction on the left and go downhill through a small jumble of rocks.

At mile 1 a short connector goes left to join the Buckeye and Bayleaf Trails. Stay right. The stone wall you parallel separates two distinct properties — the park with its fine stands of oak, the other (when I went through) with its several burn piles of oaks. The live oaks here may be the finest in the park. Milkmaids, called the first wildflower of spring, may appear among the grasses in the dead of winter.

The large meadow at 1¼ miles holds many rodents to attract such raptors as the red-tailed and sharp-shinned hawks and the kestrel. The stone wall splits into two segments and gracefully disappears over the hills south and southeast. Stay right at another connector to the Buckeye Trail. Mount George and West Sugarloaf to the northeast and Mount Veeder and Mount St. John to the west are your landmarks. The trail veers off the crest to climb a hill of chaparral with coffeeberry and coyote brush.

Begin a major nosedive at 1½ miles and cross Passini Road before 1¾ miles. Follow the sign that points uphill. Round the shoulder and traverse precipitous cliffs of Marie Creek Canyon. You come to a confusing three-way junction. To the left is a connector to the Buckeye Trail. The

Lake Louise

right fork is blocked by logs. Take the middle fork uphill, parallel a fence south, and soon top out into magnificent oak grassland. In the vicinity of mile 2 are ancient live oaks 300 to 400 years old. Just beyond is a huge bay laurel with a dozen trunks from half a foot to 1½ feet in diameter each.

Stay right at the Buckeye Trail junction at 2¼ miles and enter dense oak/bay forest with wood fern understory. Stay right again at a connector to the Lake Marie Road and come to the remains of the so-called Sea Captain's House at 2⅜ miles. The cottage may once have been a superintendent's retreat but by 1918 it was called the Watchman's Bungalow. The keeper of the dam lived here, enjoying a lake view from his wraparound porch. By 1920 when his duties ended, it was dismantled and rebuilt on the hospital grounds.

Stay to the right at another connector to Lake Marie Road. Follow an old roadbed around the lake. The hillside is a solid mass of wood ferns. At 2½ miles is the last connector to Lake Marie Road. Cross Marie Creek above the lake inlet at 2⅞ miles with giant alders overhead. Take note of the Chaparral Trail junction soon after — it's a good loop return. For the first time, you are at creek level, the bay/alder riparian overstory always cool on a hot day. Pass a junction with the newly completed Rim Rock Trail. It makes a much more rigorous return loop. Cross a series of sloping meadows where the trail is a muddy mess in winter from horse, bike, and hiker traffic. At 3½ miles you come to an unlocked green gate. You can turn around here or continue on to hike the Napa/Solano Ridge Trail Loop (see below), part of the Bay Area Ridge Trail (BART). Plans call for BART to eventually continue on to Green Valley, Rockville Hills Park and Benicia.

NAPA-SOLANO RIDGE TRAIL

DISTANCE:	1⅓ mile loop
GRADE:	Easy, but it takes a 4-mile moderate trek to reach the trailhead
BEST TIME:	All year

TRAIL NOTES:

This new trail begins at the end of the Skyline Trail, adding up to a 10-mile round trip so plan a full day and bring plenty of snacks and water. Napa-Solano Ridge Trail provides a natural extension of the Bay Area Ridge Trail. We hope that it will some day be extended to cross the county line, pass the beautiful Vallejo Lakes, and continue on to Rockville Hills Park in Green Valley.

Your trail starts at the green gate, formerly the park boundary as indicated by a gate just upslope, with an obsolete sign stating "end of property." Not far beyond the green gate stands a Bay Area Ridge Trail signpost. The loop may be done in either direction. This trail description turns right, goes down to the creek and crosses the new bridge. This is a modular fiberglass bridge, brought here in no more than 90-pound sections, designed to be strong and long lasting. Start climbing a bit with ferns and spring milkmaids at your feet and laurel forest overhead. At 1/5 mile pass through a second green gate and close it behind you.

Here the trail is an easement and private property owners have graciously granted hikers access, so please stay on the trail to respect their rights. This new trail is a natural extension of the Skyline Trail.

Cross under power lines at 1/3 mile then make a graceful, sweeping turn around a fine live oak at a grassy meadow. Soon you pass a few more picturesque swards, or glades, under large oak and bay trees that might tempt a hiker to linger. Traverse eastwards through an extensive patch of coyote brush that requires biennial trail maintenance for this fast growing shrub. In fact, the trail will get upkeep twice a year for three to five years until it becomes a stable part of the landscape.

Enter a live oak forest at 1/2 mile shielding edible miner's lettuce at its feet in spring. On the left is a curiosity, a dozen or more young bay trees scattered under oaks with no obvious dispersal tree in sight. Their seeds were most likely brought here by birds or squirrels. When you come to a fence, head downhill, first through coyote brush, then oak

136

forest, while the trail makes sweeping turns, arriving at the creek again at ¾ mile and crossing another new bridge of the same make.

In a clearing to the right are two young valley oaks in deer proof wire cages. These, and four more at the lower bridge, were planted in conjunction with a grant from the Coastal Conservancy. Come to an expansive grassy meadow, once a homestead site. Before crossing the next small stream, an historic rock wall on the right harbors a red-flowering currant bush that has exquisitely sculpted pink flowers in spring, a favorite of hummingbirds. Come to another BART signpost at one mile and merge with a wider track. Now, remember to congratulate yourself on persevering to the end of the park, because out here is a bit far for the average hiker. Continue paralleling the creek when a second track heads up and to the right onto private property. Cross under the same power lines as before, this time on the opposite side of the creek. To the west is a snapshot of Sugarloaf Peak. You return to the first green gate at 1⅓ miles and loop's end.

ADDITIONAL TRAILS

MANZANITA TRAIL

DISTANCE: 1⅝ miles one way
GRADE: Easy
BEST TIME: Winter, spring

The trail begins just beyond the park entrance by the kiosk. It skirts the archery range and Camp Coombs, then follows south-facing chaparral slopes to the east side trails junction. It can be uncomfortably warm in summer.

TOYON TRAIL

DISTANCE: 1¼ miles one way
GRADE: Easy
BEST TIME: Winter, spring

Take Manzanita Trail ⅓ mile to the turnoff. This short, vague overgrown section rejoins Manzanita after ¼ mile. Continue on Manzanita/Toyon to ⅝ mile. At this point you are above the housing at Camp Coombs. Look closely for the unsigned Toyon Trail marked by a blue ribbon. Go right and downhill following other blue ribbon markers. Before ¾ mile ignore another trail blocked by brush that leads downhill to Camp Coombs and private property. From here the Toyon Trail should be clearer. You pass above Little Yosemite and join Manzanita Trail at 1¼ miles.

BUCKEYE TRAIL

DISTANCE: 2 miles one way
GRADE: Moderate
BEST TIME: All year

Take the fenced corridor between Lakes Camille and Louise to the two-way trail junction. Turn right and find the newly rerouted start of Buckeye Trail after ⅛ mile. It traverses north-facing hillsides and joins Skyline Trail before Lake Marie, a well designed and maintained trail featuring a remarkable buckeye forest, beautiful open meadow and steep fern-covered canyon walls. This is one of my favorites.

OAKLEAF TRAIL

DISTANCE: ½ mile one way
GRADE: Easy

From the trailhead, take Lake Marie Road ¼ mile to the junction. Oakleaf Trail rejoins Lake Marie Road before the Fig Tree.

BAYLEAF TRAIL

DISTANCE: ⅝ mile one way
GRADE: Easy
BEST TIME: Spring, summer

Take Lake Marie Road ⅞ mile to the junction near the

Fig Tree. Bayleaf is a moderate climb beside an intermittent stream through oak/bay woodland. Lake Marie/Bayleaf/Skyline trails make a fine 2½-mile loop.

PASSINI ROAD

DISTANCE: ⅓ mile one way

Take Lake Marie Road 1 mile. Passini is a badly eroded right-of-way into private property. It can be used as a good connector to the Skyline Trail if you wish to avoid that trail's initial steep climb.

UPPER MARIE CREEK TRAIL

Bike and horse bypass

DISTANCE: 1⅛ miles one way
GRADE: Moderate
BEST TIME: Spring, summer, fall

Take either Manzanita Trail, Toyon Trail or Lake Marie Road to the start of Upper Marie Creek Trail at the east side trail junction. Follow the creek, then turn left and uphill at ½ mile. A fine rocky knoll-top meadow with buckeye and scrub oak perched above Marie Creek Canyon at ¾ mile offers a good picnic site. At mile 1 an unmarked junction leads you left on Chaparral Trail or right across the old spillway to the dam top.

LOWER MARIE CREEK TRAIL

DISTANCE: 1¾ miles one way
GRADE: Moderate
BEST TIME: Spring, summer, fall. In winter creek crossings
                 may be washed out.

Take Lake Marie Road for ¼ mile to the water trough where a sign reads "Marie Creek Trail, Hikers only." The first mile of this pleasant hike may be difficult to find but it also has a high solitude probability. It wanders along a blufftop between Marie Creek and Lake Marie Road. Remember to generally stay high. Only near the end of the first mile do you approach creek level.

From the water trough, drop down and to the right. You pass a hand-dug spring in the hillside, then another. Stay right at a junction and ascend. (Don't descend the prominent path — it leaves the park.) The grassy trail is indistinct for a while, close to Lake Marie Road. It connects with a wide grassy track briefly, then returns to a narrower trail.

At another junction, resist the urge to descend but stay right, passing another hand-dug spring. Ascend to meadows, then enter woods along the bluff. You get nice views here of 'Little Yosemite.' Follow blue flag markers uphill and pass over the tops of some rock outcrops. Go uphill through chaparral and pass through a low rock wall.

Descend to creek level and walk into a flat area where Stonehenge-like pedestals of rock reside under giant bay trees, one of the park's treasures. You have two choices here. Follow the trail to the Fig Tree, or cross the creek to pick up the end of Manzanita Trail. Either way takes you to the east side, four-way junction. Relax now — routefinding is simple from here. Follow the same route as for Upper Marie Creek Trail for ½ mile, then bear right to continue along the creek. After the fourth creek crossing, a sign points uphill. The trail becomes faint. Stay right at a faint connector path, then join Upper Marie Creek Trail. It's ⅛ mile to Chaparral Trail.

CHAPARRAL TRAIL

DISTANCE: ⅜ mile one way
GRADE: Easy

Take either Marie Creek Trail or Lake Marie Road to the dam. It is signed only at the north end of the dam top. This short, narrow and, in places, rough trail affords the best view of Lake Marie. Use caution on steep slopes and slick rock. It connects with Skyline Trail above the lake inlet.

ROCKVILLE HILLS REGIONAL PARK

DIRECTIONS: From the south take Interstate 80 to Suisun Valley Road near Fairfield. Travel north to Rockville Road. Turn left (west) and go about a mile to the main entrance. A second entrance is .25 mile up Rockville Road.

A charming alternate from Napa takes the Monticello Road (Highway 121) to Wooden Valley Road. Turn right on Wooden Valley Road which becomes Suisun Valley Road, then meets Rockville Road.

FEE: $2/person, $1/dog. Six-month passes available, ranging from $7-$30

HOURS/RULES: Dawn to dusk. Temporary closures possible in summer due to fire danger, in winter due to muddy trails. No horses. Bicyclists must stay on trails, wear helmets, and yield to hikers. No swimming or wading.

DISTANCE: A hike around the park's perimeter is about 6 miles. Total trail mileage is 25 miles.

GRADE: Easy to moderate

BEST TIME: Spring for wildflowers but nice all year.

DOGS ALLOWED On leash

INFO: Park Ranger Tuesday-Saturday 707/428-7614. City of Fairfield 707/428-7400. Rockville Hills Regional Park, 707/421-1351 or 432-0150

SUGGESTIONS: Weekends are extremely popular, so visit on weekdays if you want a quieter experience. Interested in maintaining trails or other volunteer work? The City of Fairfield offers three distinct types of volunteer opportunities. Join Ranger Teri Luchini for regularly held hikes and/or trail workdays.

Roy Mason knows cows. His family has run cattle in the Green Valley area since 1932. Besides owning vast acreage, he has grazing rights to the park during winter months. Mason likes to emphasize that well managed cattle do no harm to the land. Cows tend to contour graze a hillside. A good rancher will encourage this with contour fencing. But don't they eat the wildflowers, you say? On the contrary, the best place for wildflowers is thin, rocky soils where grass cover grows thinly. Thick grass cover will compete with flowers for sunlight and nutrients. For evidence, come out to Rockville Hills in March, April and May. The park has spectacular displays of nearly one hundred wildflower species. The key factor for abundant wildflowers is the quantity and timing of winter rains, the heavier and earlier the better.

According to Mason, his father bought several thousand acres from the Pierce family, one of the largest California landowners at the time, who went broke in the depression. About 1934 the Masons constructed a levee and the large stock pond was created. A right-of-way for the large utility towers you see on the property was granted before World War II. Every winter woodcutters lived on the property in small cabins to cut firewood. Cutting was selective, and done solely with hand tools. Some of the old hollow stumps are still visible. Of the very large trees, only their branches were cut. A keen eye can spot these regrowths today.

In the late 1950s a developer envisioned Rockville as

a golf course. Irrigation lines were laid and two pumps were installed at the lower stock pond. Public sympathies for open space prevailed, and the property was sold to the City of Fairfield in 1968. Rockville Hills is now a popular regional park of 630 acres, with up to 600 visitors on a busy weekend. A 1½-mile stretch of trail from the North Trailhead to the Green Valley Trailhead is dedicated as part of the Bay Area Ridge Trail.

Many of the goals of the park's Management Plan have

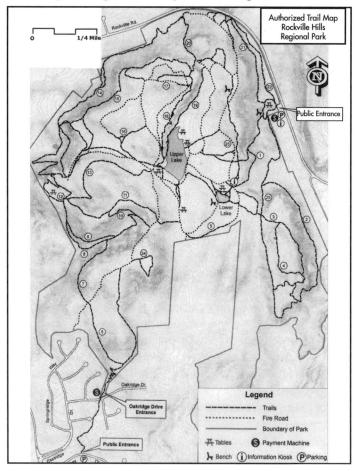

Hikers pass under gnarled limb

been implemented since the previous edition. This plan actively focuses on preserving and restoring Rockville's four plant communities — chaparral, oak woodland, grassland savanna, and aquatic habitats. Cattle have been keeping the fuel load down in the grasslands for years, but recently goats have been used in the chaparral community. In 2004 and 2006, 800 goats were supervised by a full-time shepherd to reduce fire danger without overgrazing. In the oak woodlands, although Sudden Oak Death has not appeared here, a monitoring program will soon be implemented for this disease. Two phases of invasive weed abatement have been completed by the Sacramento Conservation Corps. Both the lower and upper lakes and their ephemeral stream have been restored by Citation Northern Restoration. A key component of the plan is keeping the cattle off the sensitive edges of the lakes and streams with fencing and by installing water troughs. Restoration plantings are expected to take hold in about five years. The success of the plan can already be measured by the return of wood ducks and American kestrels to the lower lake.

144

TRAIL NOTES:

Rockville's many trails lend themselves to wandering at will and whim. Most people take the road to the upper lake (½ mile) in the center of the park. A near perfect place for a picnic, it has several tables placed around the lake shore. High tension transmission towers are the only things that seem out of place. The lake is surrounded by grass hills peppered with blue oak and buckeye. Waterfowl like geese, mallards and coots glide the shallow water. From here trails branch everywhere.

The west side of the park is a bit more remote, more lush than most west-facing hillsides in California. Look for large specimens of live oak and black oak, views of Green Valley, Elkhorn Peak, and Twin Sisters on Vaca Ridge. A well preserved stone fence is part of the northern park boundary. Underneath volcanic cliffs pocked with caves is lush undergrowth laced with poison oak (one old oak was choked with the largest poison oak trunk I've ever seen, about one half foot in diameter).

As with Rome, all trails lead to the lake. Even for those with no sense of direction, it's impossible to get lost for long, so relax and enjoy.

Hiker passes wind-sculpted bay tree at Lynch Canyon
— see next chapter.

145

LYNCH CANYON-
NEWELL OPEN SPACE

Exciting new park offers rolling grasslands, oaks, views

DIRECTIONS: From the city of Napa drive south on Highway 29 to American Canyon. Turn left and drive all the way through American Canyon until meeting Highway 80. Do not enter the freeway but cross the overpass and turn left at the McGary frontage road. Drive 1.5 miles north toward Fairfield, look for the Lynch Canyon sign, and turn left under the freeway to the entrance.

FEE: $6/day, trail maps available at kiosk

HOURS: Wednesday-Sunday, 8 a.m. to posted closing time

DISTANCE: A minimum loop trail would be about 2⅞ miles, a maximum about 7 to 8 miles. If you include the Newell Open Space loop add more.

GRADE: Moderate

ELEVATION GAIN: 500 feet

BEST TIME: Spring, fall

MULTIUSE TRAILS: Hikers, bicyclists and equestrians welcome. Dogs are not permitted, leashed or not.

WARNING: Dress for possible high winds on the ridges and muddy trails in winter and spring.

SUGGESTIONS: Volunteer Trail Care Days occur the second Saturday of every month. Contact land steward Ken Poerner at 707/580-6277 or ken@solanolandtrust.org
No official entrance exists for Newell Open

Space on the Napa side. It can only be reached from Lynch Canyon at this time. Contact Community Services Department of the City of American Canyon for more information, 707/648-7275.

The first known use of Lynch Canyon dates to at least 4,000 years B.C. This land was used but not settled by the Suisune tribe of Patwin Native Americans, part of a larger linguistic group known as Wintun. They were skilled hunter-gatherers, taking advantage of the rich and diverse plant and animal life. Four acorn grinding sites have been documented in Lynch. In prehistoric times coast live oak and interior live oak trees were more numerous than now. A lack of middens at these acorn grinding sites means they came here to hunt and gather but lived in villages elsewhere.

This area was a virtual Garden of Eden then, supporting large predators like bear, mountain lion and coyote and large herbivores like elk, mule deer and antelope. These latter three animals roamed the area in large herds numbering in the thousands. They were easy on the native bunch grasses, which covered these hillsides until the European invasion.

Starting with the Mexican period in 1769, elk, antelope, bear, and mountain lion were eliminated or became scarce. When General Vallejo purchased these lands in 1843 from the Mexican governor of California for $5,000, he began grazing domesticated animals like cattle and sheep. His lands, stretching from present day Sonoma County through Napa and into Solano County, held upwards of 100,000 animals. They soon began to trample and exterminate the native grasses, and combined with the drought of the 1860s it is believed the conversion to exotics became widespread in that decade. Wood was the only source for heating and cooking in those days so that oaks were cut at a fast pace. When they became scarce, the eucalyptus tree was brought from Australia. Eucalyptus didn't make the most desirable firewood but they served for shade and windbreaks and now serve as habitat for owls and hawks.

After 1862, Vallejo's claim to the land was invalidated by the U.S. courts and the land was subdivided into two parcels. A number of subsistence farmer families lived on the upper and lower homesteads over the years. Cattle and sheep raising was the main use with vegetable gardens and orchard fruits to supplement their diet. Large orchards were never planted due to the cool nature of the climate here. Lynch Canyon is well supplied with spring water, and the development of these water sources for drinking water, stock watering and crop irrigation has never dried up, even in drought years. In the 1950s a reservoir was created, then enlarged in the 1970s. It is planned to reduce the capacity of the water body due to poor quality of the work during the dam enlargement.

In the 1980s a new land use potential threatened to change the nature of this area irrevocably. Tri-County Development bought both parcels in 1983-84 with the intent to fill the south fork of Lynch Creek with garbage mostly from San Francisco. This landfill proposal was defeated by the Cordelia Homeowners Association in a ballot measure in November 1984. In the nineties Tri County sold the land to Solano County Farmlands and Open Space Foundation for $4.2 million.

Lynch Canyon is now safe from any development other than minor improvements to receive the recreational public. A parking lot, restroom, informational display case, fencing, hiking trails and picnic tables are installed. Cattle grazing still occurs on these 1039 acres of permanent open space. There is still a fine diversity of habitats supporting deer, fox, bobcat, waterfowl and raptors including the golden eagle, which is relatively abundant. Lynch is home to a federally listed threatened species, the California red-legged frog. It

148

is adjacent to Newell Open Space of Napa County, which is accessible by hiking trail from this side only.

TRAIL NOTES:

Lynch Canyon offers almost 10 miles of trail (add 3 miles more for the Newell Loop) on 1,039 acres of steep rolling hills and gentle valleys. Two forks of Lynch Creek drain this watershed and flow into Suisun Marsh. Plant communities include grassland, evergreen oak woodland, and wetland marsh. An ideal hike would pass through all these habitats in a loop that includes the Prairie Ridge Trail. Up on the ridgetops are outstanding views of the Bay Area and excellent photographic opportunities. The wind blows here most days quite strongly and the wind-sculpted bay trees that cling to rocky outcrops on top serve aesthetic purposes as well as shelter for the hiker. Three Bay Area prominences, Mount Tamalpais, Mount Diablo and Mount St. Helena are all visible. When the morning or afternoon sunlight dances and glitters on the bay waters, it's a dazzling sight. A clear day will give you a visual perspective from San Francisco to the Sierra Nevada.

Cultural features of interest are the old Lynch homestead site, demolished in February 2007, on Lynch Road near the start. You can still see evidence left from those days like a water trough, corral, orchards and large shade trees like cypress and eucalyptus, the latter a known site for golden eagle nesting. The upper homestead located near Saddle Trail was built in the 1860s and abandoned in the 1930s. A year-round spring was no doubt a key factor in the choice of site. What appears to have been a cold storage building sits next to it. The barn and house are gone except for the stone walls, but across the creek is a tin roofed structure once used as a chicken coop. A second home site with only the stone foundation left today was burned in the extensive grass fire of 1966. Upslope is a windbreak of 100-year-old eucalyptus and one Monterey cypress. Other eucalyptus windbreaks on

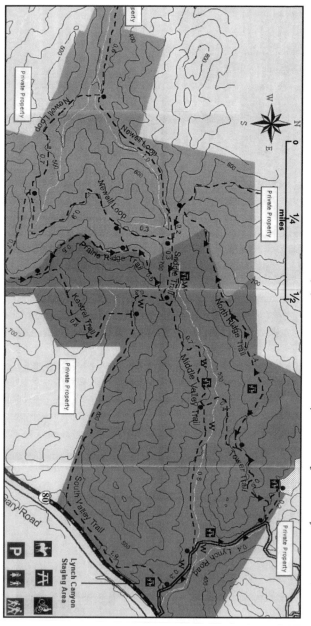

Map courtesy of Solano Land Trust, produced by Green Info Network, 2007

the preserve serve as habitat for the great horned owl.

The recommended short loop begins at the staging area and follows Lynch Road to the reservoir. Take a short detour here to watch waterfowl by a picnic site. Then take the Tower Trail connector over to the Middle Valley Trail and back to the start. This loop is slightly less than 3 miles.

The recommended long loop begins with Lynch Road to the Tower Trail, then continues up the Middle Valley Trail to visit the upper homestead site. Then take the Saddle Trail to the Prairie Ridge Trail and the preserve's high point. The Kestrel Trail drops steeply to the South Valley Trail where you have two choices. Return via the Middle Valley Trail or by the South Valley Trail along the south perimeter. The last mile of the South Valley Trail parallels the freeway closely. Either way it is just over 6 miles.

Indian grinding rock in Upper Lynch Canyon

STEBBINS COLD CANYON RESERVE

A part of the University of California Natural Reserve System

Cold Canyon has received more attention in recent years both from U.C. Davis Reserve researchers and administrators and from the general public. Improvement of existing trails, a new loop trail, and new signage all mean that this area can now be highly recommended and is perhaps one of the best short hike areas in the region. Trails here are well used and probably most popular with Yolo County residents.

DIRECTIONS:	From Rutherford take Highway 128, or from Napa take Highway 121, to Moskowite Corners. Continue on Highway 128 to Monticello Dam. You will make a short descent to a sweeping bend in the road where Cold Creek passes under Cold Creek Bridge. Park at the large turnout on the left (north). The trail starts at a silver gate on the south side of the road.
DISTANCE:	4¾ miles round trip
GRADE:	Mostly moderate, except strenuous on the 'steps'
ELEVATION GAIN:	1,500 feet
BEST TIME:	Spring, fall
INFO:	U. C. Davis, 530/752-6949
WARNING:	Area subject to mud slides in winter
SUGGESTIONS:	Bring binoculars for views of the Sierra Nevada and Mount Lassen. If you're sure you want to hike the whole loop, take the turnoff to Blue Ridge Trail near the start because new

trail switchbacks make the ascent to the ridge easier this way. In this report, the trail is described to the Homestead first as most people will take this route and return.
Pleasants Ridge Trail climbs one mile to views.

Kentucky pioneer John Reid Wolfskill took possession of *Rancho Rio de los Putos* near Winters in 1842. Part of his land extended along Putah Creek close to Devil's Gate, but Cold Canyon was just outside the rancho boundaries. Because he refused to become a Mexican citizen, the grant was actually made in his brother William's name. John Wolfskill was the founder of the horticulture industry in the Sacramento Valley. Some of his original fruit tree cuttings came from George Yount's *Rancho Caymus*.

A year later the Berryessa brothers, Jose and Sisto, were given their own Mexican land grant of 35,000 acres, later known as the *Rancho de las Putas*. It was the largest piece of land ever given in Napa County, covering most of Berryessa Valley. According to California historian Erwin Gudde, the Indian name *Putah* preserves the name of the branch of Patwin Indians who lived on its banks. He states that its similarity to the Spanish word *puta* (meaning harlot) is purely coincidental. A contrasting story circulates that employees of the Berryessas would go down to Putah Canyon to purchase Indian women for trinkets. Legend has it that the brothers Berryessa lost their land (at 25 cents per acre) chiefly to horse-race gambling debts.

The principal owners by 1866 were John Lawley, William Hamilton and J.H. Bostwick who made a killing by subdividing Berryessa Valley into small farms. A portion in the south was set aside for a town. The building of Monticello began the same year when E.A. Peacock erected the first hotel. Soon there were homes, a blacksmith shop, two general

153

stores, more hotels, saloons and a cemetery. Eventually this farming community held about 200 people.

Agricultural emphasis changed from cattle to wheat. Wheat grew fast and rich due to the climate and the valley's soil, fifty per cent of which was later rated as Class 1 Yolo loam (very fertile). Getting wheat to market was another matter. Only two roads led out of this isolated valley. One, often flooded in the wet months, went down narrow Putah Canyon to Winters and the Sacramento Valley. The other was a brutal, two-day haul by mule wagon to Napa.

California's agriculture began to diversify about the time

The flooding of Berryessa Valley

"Under the swelling pressure of a skyrocketing birth rate, places for people to live and water for crops and factories has become critical . . . bulldozers are only slightly slower than atomic bombs . . . the nature of destruction is not altered by calling it the price of progress. To witness population inflation of such proportions that ways of life are uprooted, fruiting trees sawed down, productive land inundated and bodies already buried forced out of the ground is to realize that as life teems so does death. And that man is the active agent of both."
From the inside front cover of Death of a Valley, *by Dorothea Lange and Pirkle Jones, a pictorial chronicle of the last year of Berryessa Valley.*

It was common knowledge from the late 1800s that Devil's Gate at the head of Putah Canyon would make an ideal dam site. As early as 1906 engineers were casting covetous eyes that way. It wasn't until 1948 that a bill to authorize dam construction appeared before Congress. That bill never passed, but the Secretary of the Interior exercised his independent power and gave it the go ahead. It was the only federal dam project ever approved in this way. Strong objection and attempted litigation by Napa County was fruitless.

the wheat market weakened in the 1880s. Farmers slowly changed over to fruit growing, chiefly pears and grapes, by 1920. A small scale oil drilling business was run in the 1920s by a man named Griffiths. He lost financial backers in the depression and the fledgling business never recovered.

In Cold Canyon a Greek named John Vlahos was granted an ownership patent in 1938 to graze goats and cattle. According to the rules of the Homestead Act of 1862, he needed to have begun improvements five years earlier. To raise collateral for his mortgage of $2,500, he made 2,000 pounds of cheese which he stored in a cold storage building

With tactics similar to the Owens Valley land buyout by Los Angeles at the turn of the century, federal authorities offered farmers prices far below market value for their property. Facing eminent domain, landowners in Berryessa Valley had little choice but to sell. Many would never find land again at comparable cost. During the final year of 1956, a few houses were moved to higher ground. The rest were burned. All trees were ordered cut to within six inches of the ground, including ancient valley oaks, landmarks for centuries to the Indians, Spanish and Americans. Bodies were disinterred from Monticello Cemetery and moved to Spanish Flat. The only structure left intact was the Putah Creek Bridge. Quarried from local sandstone, at 217 feet it was called the largest stone bridge west of the Rockies. Today it is buried under 160 feet of water.

Much to everyone's surprise, heavy rains quickly filled Berryessa Valley that first winter. Under the rising waters, one-sixth of Napa County's farming acreage disappeared. Tax revenues lost are estimated at $800,000 per year. Lake Berryessa is solely on Napa County land, yet none of its water benefitted the county (Solano County farms are the main beneficiaries). Although not an original objective, recreation soon became popular. Now bass fishing, water skiing, swimming, board sailing and house boating are enjoyed through the year.

located in a shady, stream side location near his home. The name Cold Canyon originates with this cold storage unit. The remains of the road he built to transport his goods to market is now the main hiking trail.

Between 1979 and 1984, Vlahos' land was acquired by the University of California for the purpose of preserving the land for teaching and research. It was named in honor of Dr. G. Ledyard Stebbins, a professor of genetics at UC Davis. One of thirty-three Reserves in the UC system, it is also one of the few that allows public access. Plant and animal communities in these 640 acres are largely intact and hold a healthy number of species. For example, there are over 200 species of butterflies and moths here alone. The animals you're most likely to sight or see sign of include mule deer, quail, hawks, wild turkey, coyote, bobcat, wood rats, ground squirrels, newts, and some of the ten species

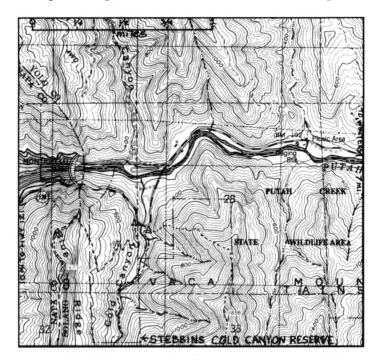

of snakes (only one venomous). To learn more about this well-studied area, visit the Stebbins site online at http://nrs. ucdavis.edu/stebbins.html.

TRAIL NOTES:

Just inside the gate the trail forks to the left for Pleasants Ridge Trail. Stay right. Look for small trail signs starting with the number 01 after you pass the gate. The Homestead Trail stays on the east side of Cold Creek for the first ½ mile. Quickly you come to an eastern tributary. Although its watershed is small, the floodwaters of 1995 raised havoc here. Most of the riparian vegetation in the creek below was stripped away along with a great deal of soil that, combined with the raging waters, nearly took out the highway too. Since then tons of debris have been removed from the trail, and the streambed is rebounding with plant life. You may see shooting stars and the shocking magenta flowers of redbud around March and April. To the right is the Blue Ridge Loop trail junction.

At ⅕ mile you enter the Reserve proper and pass through a new gate to a new display case packed with great information. Staff at the U.C. Reserve system are very active here at Stebbins, leading guided hikes and training hike leaders. It is an active ecological study area for students and teachers at U.C. Davis. Please leave study areas undisturbed. Pass a tall, classic looking gray pine (Pinus sabiniana), and then the trail negotiates a short hill with sturdy water bars. At ⅓ mile you cross over another small hillock that came down as a land slump with many plants intact. In February, shiny brown seeds of the buckeye litter the ground, sending out pale white roots. All along the trail later in spring are wildflowers like brodiaea, monkeyflower, Indian paintbrush, white flowered yarrow and yerba santa, western wallflower and golden fairy lantern. To the west is a prominent rocky peak on Blue Ridge that often hosts hawks circling overhead, and its sheltered ledges are ideal nesting sites for the turkey vulture.

Before the crossing of Cold Creek, look for a side trail to the right marked by a scrub oak. The creek here is a good place to see the Pacific tree frogs or yellow-legged frogs whose calls you may have been hearing. A large boulder at trail's end has a rounded hole or mortar made by Patwin Native Americans for grinding acorns to flour. Back on the main trail at ½ mile you come to Cold Creek. If it is moderately high you may find a dry, rock hop crossing fifty feet upstream on the left, or enjoy the plunge on a warm day. Start the ascent to the homestead now and at ¾ mile cross over a serpentine spring on a miniature wooden bridge.

The trail climbs steadily above the creek through dense chaparral species like ceanothus and mountain mahogany (Cercocarpus). The trail veers south to follow what looks like a tributary of Cold Creek, but a glance at the map shows you are still on Cold Creek. What I believe is going on is a nomenclature anomaly. The larger Wild Horse Creek, which joins Cold Creek below, has been given tributary status by mistake. According to standards set by the Geographic Board, the waters running into Putah Creek should be called Wild Horse Creek. But local usage and custom are strong and to correct it would only cause further confusion.

Walk steeply through a brushy section that can be a virtual tunnel if left unpruned. On my hike the tunnel was cleared back and regularly spaced water bars installed to prevent erosion. Just beyond, a sign stating "no entry please" requests hikers to stay off a fragile hillside. On these soils even a small informal trail can lead to a major landslide. Soon, on the left side of the trail is the Vlahos homestead near some meadows (probably cleared for goat grazing) and an enormous, many branched gray pine. All that's left of the home is a low stone wall, an old well and some rusted junk.

At 1¼ miles is the turnoff for the loop hike. But first, don't miss the cold house that has given Cold Creek its name. Continue by crossing a small tributary, go down and cross Cold Creek to see the slightly better preserved stone walls of the cold storage building used by Vlahos to store his goat cheese. Big oaks, maples and bays make sure this delightful place is always cool and shady. You may follow the creek a short distance to a waterfall and pool for wading or observing aquatic life.

BLUE RIDGE LOOP

Return to the loop trail junction unsigned at press time, marked by a hunk of rusted metal rife with holes like it was Swiss cheese. Head up and left through oak and bay forest following old galvanized pipe. Go through some chaparral undergrowth then return to the creek. You will climb a few railroad tie steps then return to creek side again at 1½ miles. Now begin a short but strenuous section of trail gaining 800 feet in ¼ mile. It's a real quad burner but just pretend you're on your Stairmaster with the bonus of better air quality and views. The trail will employ both short switchbacks and 176 high steps between here and the ridgetop.

At 1¾ miles step out of a chamise thicket into the open for great views of Pleasants Ridge. The trail splits at an un-

Monticello Dam, completed 1957

marked junction. Take the right fork and soon splendid views emerge to the west of Lake Berryessa, Cedar Roughs, Mount St. Helena, Cobb Mountain, and Mount Konocti. Pass a high-maintenance chaparral section, then around mile 2 you will see the first of several perfect sandstone outcroppings ideal for a break or lunch. As the trail rises and falls on the ridgetop over various peaklets, look east through the gap of Devil's Gate and see on a clear winter or spring day not only the city of Davis but a snow covered Sierra Nevada, with Mount Lassen to the north.

Around 2¼ miles I found myself in a seeming dead end. If this happens to you, back up a bit and look for a sandstone slot to shinny up. Distant Snow Mountain and Goat Mountain come into view as you negotiate interesting passages over rock interspersed with bits of trail. Soon the homestead will be directly below. At 2½ miles look directly along Blue Ridge to Berryessa Peak, then descend another peaklet. The trail will become distinctly easier now, the former high point of the old trail. Watch for the trail tread to totally disappear as it takes a sharp left turn over a sandstone ledge. The ridgetop is a great place to observe raptors close up. At a low point in the ridge they will come sweeping just above the tops of the chaparral as they cross from one canyon to the next.

At mile 3 the trail charges bravely up a steep crumbly ridge, tops out and turns briefly toward the lakeside of the ridge. For photographers, look for another massive sandstone slab that provides foreground interest for a lake shot. Hang a right and you're on the east side again. A series of long switchbacks avoids a former environmentally destructive gully trail. Beyond 3¼ miles an unmarked side trail leads to a don't miss dramatic overlook of the lake, Devil's Gate, and Monticello Dam. Watch your footing extremely carefully here due to loose rock and big drop-offs.

Get back on the main trail and enjoy the last mile. It's easy going on the new switchbacks, sometimes over industrial size water bars placed here to minimize erosion on this highly erodable slope. About the time you hear the creek again at 4½ miles, the trail splits. You can take the left fork on the fire road back to the highway, covered in landslide debris for years but now cleaned up, or the right fork heading down to the creek then up to the beginning of the loop.

KNOXVILLE WILDLIFE AREA

Vast new Knoxville Wildlife Area offers abundant hiking choices

Knoxville Wildlife Area has only recently dropped onto the hiker's horizon of possibilities. Found in remote eastern Napa County west of Blue Ridge, the area is bisected by both Etiquera Creek and the only major access road in the area, Knoxville Berryessa Road. Knoxville Wildlife Area began modestly as a 93-acre donation in 1988 as habitat preserve, but in 2000 Homestake Mining Company sold 8,000 acres to the California Department of Fish and Game as part of its closure of the nearby McLaughlin gold mine. Then in 2005, the Napa Ranch of 12,000 plus acres was acquired, including the Zem Zem Canyon area. This 20,000-acre wonderland in the Putah Creek watershed includes chaparral, oak, grassland, and riparian communities with fabulous wildlife viewing opportunities. It protects rare and endemic species of plants and insects specifically adapted to the serpentine soils abundantly found here. Knoxville Wildlife Area is part of the much larger Blue Ridge-Berryessa Natural Area of Napa, Lake, Colusa and Yolo counties, encompassing 800,000 acres of wild, natural, agricultural and recreational lands, both public and private, a partnership managed by BLM, Bureau of Reclamation, Fish and Game, and the UC Natural Reserve System.

Knoxville is former cattle country and the many ranch roads now serve as access trails for hikers, hunters, birders, fishers and wildlife enthusiasts. Some of the many animals that live here are mountain lion, black tailed deer, Rio Grande wild turkeys, and raptors such as owls, hawks, eagles and falcons. Many of the trailheads

162

are unsigned at press time and explorers can discover many more hikes than the two great ones described in this chapter. Car camping facilities do not yet exist, but backpacking or primitive camping is allowed ¼ mile beyond parking areas. Bring your own water or purify all water sources. Hunting is allowed in season.

History of Zem Zem

Just looking at the place one would never know that the two acres of flat, high ground to the right of the trail-head, between Etiquera Creek and Zem Zem Creek, was once the busy and vibrant homestead of a pioneer family in the latter part of the nineteenth century. Little evidence is left now of their home and outbuildings, orchard and shade trees, vegetable garden and guest cottages, and farther up the canyon, hay growing, sheep and cattle ranching operations. In fact, a whole community network ex-

The Owen homestead about 1910

isted in this region, propelled by the Knoxville mine six miles up the road, the fourth most successful quicksilver mine in U.S. history. Numerous families lived along the Knoxville Berryessa Road, surviving by skills most of us know nothing about. Wealthier folks came from near and far to drink and bathe in the sulphur waters, staying at the Sulphur Springs Hotel a quarter mile up the road from Zem Zem. A post office operated here for twenty-one years and mail was delivered daily, summers by stage and winters by horse rider. In the 1880s, these neighbors would get together for periodic 'shin digs,' barn dances that would last until dawn. Today, as if it were all a dream, the land is returning to its natural state under the auspices of the California Department of Fish and Game.

In 1849 Leander Owen's father was bitten by the Gold Bug. Leander, his brothers, and father Thomas made plans to leave for California, but before he left, Leander got a promise from his sweetheart, Mary Hobart, to wait for his return. She promised, but it would be four long years before she saw him again. On their overland journey they were pinned down on the Great Plains by a mass buffalo migration for thirty hours as the herd thundered by, making everything including sleep impossible. Their oxen were lost in the stampede, and it took weeks to recover them. Thirteen months were spent in the crossing before they arrived at the little pueblo of Los Angeles.

The next year they wandered north to the gold country of Tuolumne and opened a trading post near present day French Camp, which proved a steadier income than gold panning. California had become a state in 1849, and numerous land title disputes followed for many years. In 1852 the Owens lost their property in such a dispute and moved west to Suisun in Solano County. Here they bought land and grew hay, and the Owen women joined them from Illinois.

Leander returned to Illinois two years later and married his sweetheart Mary. With the oft repeated phrase, "once a Californian, always a Californian," Leander eventually convinced his wife to move west which they did in 1861. She never saw her family again. They settled again in Suisun, but

Mary's health was affected by the constant bay winds, so in July 1865, they moved up to northeastern Napa County to the newly-built Sulphur Springs Hotel near Zem Zem Creek and began working for the proprietor. The origin of the name Zem Zem, which means 'healing waters,' came from an apparently well-traveled or well-read guest who came, like others, to drink and bathe in the black sulphur waters. It is said that he commented the waters here tasted like that of the sacred springs of Mecca called by the same name. Apparently this was less than a compliment since the brackish waters of the Holy Well, like its western counterpart, are highly disagreeable for most, having been described as tasting like a "very dirty gun barrel," and by Sir Richard Burton "apt to cause diarrhea and boils and I never saw a stranger drink it without a wry face."

After two years the work became burdensome and they decided to leave the hotel, while at the same time Grandfather Thomas sold his land in Suisun and bought land in Zem Zem, including the Sulphur Springs Hotel. Thomas and his sons went into partnership, and several homes were built including the one at the confluence of Zem Zem Creek and Etiquera Creek where Leander and Mary lived. It was a sturdy cottage built for a growing family, with a wood stove in the kitchen and a great fireplace in the living room capable of taking four-foot logs. Nearby was a rambling fifty-foot long barn with an orchard of apples, plums and peaches. Also planted were a row of Osage orange trees, a sweet smelling fruit with an inedible pithy center. These trees can still be seen today soon after passing the gate at the trailhead. Mary Owen was in charge of a large vegetable garden that flourished partly because she insisted on great quantities of easily obtained barnyard manure for fertilizer. Many kinds of vegetables were grown, including the all important popcorn plant for munching after dinner on cold winter nights. Water was plentiful and was piped to the house from a white sulphur spring located in a small canyon south of the house. It was lukewarm in temperature so that baths were pleasant even in winter.

As you walk up the trail alongside Zem Zem Creek,

there are nearly a dozen 'flats' on the way to the falls. Each one of these was then planted with hay or used for cattle or sheep grazing, up to 4,000 head. Two or three homes were built in the upper canyon for family members. Sheep raising proved time consuming and expensive and eventually was phased out. In the 1880s hot springs resorts popped up everywhere in Lake County, and the Owens discovered that boarding visitors was more profitable than keeping stock. They continued to grow hay since horses were still the main form of transportation. Guests at the house paid two dollars a night or they could spend the night at Camper's Flat just off the main road at the big bend in Etiquera Creek.

Leander Owen was fond of honey, and he had a woodsman's talent for finding 'honey trees.' He would find a seep or spring and patiently wait for a bee to come by to drink. Then he would watch it carefully. If the bee came in low and heavy with pollen, he knew it would soon make a beeline for home. Quickly, he would follow the bee to its nest, then take the honey out just like a bear, sometimes using the smoke method if they got riled.

A post office was established in 1869 at the Sulphur Springs Hotel, and Carrol Owen, the successful owner and operator, became postmaster also. When he left the area in 1881, the post office duties were moved down the road to the Owens residence and taken up by Leander. Mail was delivered daily by two-horse buckboard or stagecoach in summer and by horseback in winter. In the early days a rider needed to be skillful and daring because the road crossed the creek thirty-five times in ten miles. Even today, the ten low water crossings of Eticuera can be impossible to ford by car in flood stage. When the creeks surrounding the property were high, the Owens were isolated. Leander ingeniously solved the problem of getting the mail across by rigging a pulley system that ran over the creek from the house to the road.

Perhaps the most popular community events held in the Knoxville area in the 1880s were the barn dances. Neighbors often lived far apart but the dances were well attended.

A newspaper account of the day describing one dance at the Sulphur Springs Hotel reported that people had come from Pope Valley, Napa, Woodland, Kelseyville, Knoxville, Dixon, Winters, Monticello and Capell Valley. After work on Saturday (where the expression 'hoe down' came from) and dressed in their finest, they'd hitch the horse to the wagon and travel up to ten miles of rough road when, for example, it was held at the Twichells place in Mysterious Valley. These dances were well-ordered events, with expert fiddle players, a caller, and a person to keep order, who made sure that no eligible girl sat on the sidelines. They danced Virginia reels, waltzes, the Shottiche and square and basket quadrilles. During short intermissions between dances, the young men strolled or sat with their sweethearts, keeping them cool with a large feather fan. No couple would even think in those days of 'wandering in the dell.' At midnight they all participated in a big feast, then continued dancing until dawn. After coffee and leftovers, tired and happy, they would pile into the wagon for the long ride home, to sleep the rest of the day.

In 1890 the post office ceased operations, and a year later the Owens sold their place and moved to Berryessa Valley. In a memoir written in 1948 by Leander's son Frank Owen it was reported that the house was still standing well against the elements. Ida Owen (Swift) was born at Zem Zem in 1871, was married and had her first child here also. She composed a 160-page hand written memoir in 1935 of her life and times at Zem Zem, on which this summary is based.

ZEM ZEM FALLS

DIRECTIONS: Although unmarked, the trailhead is fairly easy to find. Take Knoxville Berryessa Road along the north end of Lake Berryessa and continue into public lands. Cross over four low water crossings, then before mile marker 24 look for a turnout on the right and a green gate on the left. It's just before the fifth low

	water crossing. This is Zem Zem Trailhead.
DISTANCE:	3½ miles one way, 7 miles round trip
GRADE:	Easy except some moderate cross-country at the end
BEST TIME:	Spring
DOGS ALLOWED:	Yes
INFO:	California Department of Fish and Game, 707/944-5500
SUGGESTIONS:	There are nine creek crossings on the hike so take your water sandals or a pair of boots with water-resistant coating. You'll need them in a year of normal or higher rainfall. In the extreme low water year of 2007, we did not pull out the Tevas, even in March.
NOTE:	On many maps you will see the spelling Zim Zim Creek. I use the original spelling Zem Zem.

TRAIL NOTES:

There is no official hiker entrance yet so step over barbed wire on the left of the green gate and follow the dirt road. An overstory of valley oaks overlooks a big, lazy bend in Eticuera Creek. Soon you pass over a small tributary. A short distance up that creek is the source of Zem Zem's white sulfur springs. You may notice next to the your trail some odd thorny fruit trees with softball size, sweet but unusual smelling fruit of a yellow-orange color. They have a distinct corrugated surface that made me dub them yellow brain fruit before I discovered their real name. These are Osage orange trees planted by Leander Owen in the late 1800s. These same trees can be seen ¼ mile up the road at the site of the old Sulphur Springs Hotel. The fruit is not exactly edible but may have been used for flavoring.

The road follows the base of the hills next to a meadow filled with star thistle now. Once it flourished with the Owen's fruit orchards and vegetable gardens. In the north corner of the lot close to the confluence of Zem Zem Creek and Eticuera Creek the Owen house once stood. Come to Zem Zem Creek at ⅕ mile and the first of nine crossings. Go through a distinct slot opening in the hills into a shady canyon. The canyon opens up into the first of several big grassy meadows that grazed cattle and were home to several Owen family members. In general, but not always, the plant community distribution is such: the lowlands hold the valley oaks and grasses, midway up are the blue oaks and arching gray pines, and up high the chaparral community. You can see the effects of the most recent major fire of October 2004, the 39,000-acre Rumsey Fire.

At ½ mile is the second stream crossing. If the water is low, you can avoid getting wet by walking along a sandbar to the right then to the other side at a large oak seeming to mark the crossing. I noticed this phenomenon of the crossing oak elsewhere, an oak on the bank at the exact spot most desirable to cross. At ⅔ mile on high meadow ground is an old hunter's camp, consisting of a couple of lean-tos on the right and a smaller roofed structure on the left of the trail. A step down and closer to the creek is a wood platform and a pipe running up a stake that looks like a makeshift shower 'al fresco'. Birdsong was especially noticeable here, including the sweet warble of the meadowlark. We even heard

the laughing call of the pileated woodpecker, a species once thought to need deep woods that appears to be increasing its range. Be careful at the next small tributary crossing where you need to do a small leap over a drop off. Beyond at a junction of jeep roads, continue to follow the pleasant double track up valley.

Just before and just after mile 1 are the third and fourth stream crossings. At 1½ miles you approach a sweeping bend in the creek. Make the fifth and sixth crossings at the beginning and end of that bend. So far you've followed the regularly spaced 12-foot posts marking the right of way for a fiber optic line. It leaves us here as they now march off in another direction. You may see or hear Pacific tree frogs and mallard ducks in the creek. What you won't see are cattle, now thankfully banned from the area. The minor erosion gullies you see plugged with river stones are the work of the Department of Fish and Game.

Before 2 miles are some pools and falls in Zem Zem Creek formed by a conglomerate rock looking a little like natural concrete. Beyond 2 miles you reach the seventh ford near a major tributary. You might notice the creek get a little smaller as you enter a narrower canyon. By 2⅛ miles reach the eighth crossing, then pass an area of minor land slumping and ascend slightly into graceful blue oak woodland. Just before 3 miles is the last stream ford. You'll soon see a very large boulder blocking the left split in the road. You can take the left fork into the creek past some ruins and follow it to the falls. We ascend the right fork for the only real uphill of the trip. Pass a serpentine rock outcrop, then take the next left fork, which sports showy bush lupine in spring. Quite suddenly around 3⅛ miles you come to your first view of the falls. A second, better viewpoint for cameras with telephoto lenses lies ahead. Pass a land-slumped area and then get great views down canyon all the way to Berryessa Peak.

Before 3¾ miles turn off the road abruptly and head downhill over moderate cross-country slopes and inter-connecting footpaths. Do not try to hit the base of the falls directly but aim for a spot a hundred yards or so below that, then follow the creek the rest of the way. Look for some excellent examples of conglomerate rock consisting of many small river pebbles and one or two huge river-smoothed stones conspicuously sticking out of the smaller matrix. You'll find a superb swimming hole at the base of the 100 foot falls, so be prepared for a nice swim in the surprisingly cold, spring fed waters of this five star destination.

LONG CANYON, KNOXVILLE WILDLIFE AREA

DIRECTIONS: From St. Helena drive north on Highway 29 for 0.5 mile to Deer Park Road and turn right. Drive 8 miles to Angwin, then continue into Pope Valley. Turn right at Pope/Chiles Valley Road, take the second left, which is Pope Canyon Road. At the airstrip turn left and continue on Pope Canyon Road to the Knoxville Berryessa Road. Turn left and follow the west shore of the lake over two bridges.

After the lake, continue as the road narrows and goes into a canyon and reaches public lands. Just past Mile Marker 27.50 is an old metal corral on the right. Use the ample parking on either side of the road.

DISTANCE: 9¼-mile loop

GRADE: Moderate

ELEVATION GAIN: An easy 1,000 feet — seriously, the gain is gradual over 5 miles

BEST TIME: Spring, autumn, winter in that order

DOGS ALLOWED: Yes

WARNING: Watch for plentiful snakes on the grassy ranch roads in spring.

SUGGESTIONS: Do the loop in a counter-clockwise direction because it makes for a more pleasant hike and the elevation gain is more moderate this way.

For a shorter hike, try 'Six Dog' Trail starting at mile marker 26.50. Duck under the fence on the east side of the road and find the trail for a 5-mile loop. Have a good map and compass to find your way, good advice for any hikes in Knoxville area.

TRAIL NOTES:

Go over the green gate to the left of the corral or wind through the corral itself. You'll find the path level for the first mile. Pass through charming meadows with granddaddy oak trees and in spring, if your timing is right, the brilliant magenta blossoms of redbud. You cross a small creek a few times in the first mile and may see the western aquatic gopher snake watching you closely, all but his head submerged. At ¼ mile you pass one of many water troughs for stock no longer grazed here. It's quite common to hear the sharp cry of red-tailed hawks, or see them catching thermals over Blue Ridge.

A recent major fire has burned chaparral close by but mostly left oaks in the valley bottom untouched. At another creek crossing just before ½ mile we saw, on our hike, an active beehive inside an oak's old trail blaze. Throughout the spring it's likely you'll see the finely sculpted, tiny white flower of woodland star on its long slender stem. Beyond ½ mile you transition from a single track to an old ranch road and continue up valley. At ⅔ mile, find some old rusted metal bed frames reclining under oaks, although the campers who used them have long since departed. Before mile 1 is a small stream crossing, then just beyond is a significant and possibly confusing junction. At the offset fence line, take the left fork down to the creek, cross it, then soon begin to climb above it.

Pass through a perennially swampy area, above which is a crescent shaped, land slump scar. Wild turkey are quite common in the Knoxville hills. They may look awkward on the ground but when they fly they do it gracefully and with few wing beats. Come to a crest of sorts at 1½ miles, then at 1¾ miles reach an important junction, one to remember if you are doing the loop. At a ten-foot high round metal tank, used in the cattle ranching days for rock salt storage, the road splits. You'll be here again on the way back. Take the right fork, though it may look less traveled and/or obscured by grass. Around 2¼ miles you return to Long Creek and continue upstream. Soon you come across a large patch of wild rose with a large, 'granary' gray pine nearby, chock full of holes for woodpeckers to store acorns in.

By 3⅓ miles the canyon has narrowed and become more intimate. The creek does an 'S' turn and you cross the creek twice, quickly. If you don't need an expansive view for a lunch site this one works, but watch the red ants in the creek bed. Encounter a major washout of the road at mile 4, with just a narrow strip of tread left. Soon after, a trough full of water and aquatic plants provides habitat for frogs. These old stock watering troughs are significant habitat for declining frog populations, especially endangered species like the red-legged frog. Above, a shallow dry watershed leads up to Blue Ridge, but the trail takes an abrupt left turn.

The road climbs steeply then comes close to a spectacular overview (if you wander off road a bit) at 4¼ miles

of Blue Ridge and the Fiske Creek watershed. There is an absolutely startling contrast between the oak and grassland habitat you're in and the monoculture chaparral of

Stock pond near the top of Long Canyon

Fiske Canyon. You'll start climbing steeply now, with a view down Long Canyon to Lake Berryessa. Pass a stock pond, then at 4¾ miles reach the apex of the hike with another of those rock salt storage cylinders. Superb views are found here on the ridgetop, including Mount St. Helena and Cobb Mountain, perhaps from a less common perspective. Descend the ridge of fine blue oak woodlands, so narrow, like a spine, you can check out Long Canyon with your left eye and Foley Creek canyon with your right eye simultaneously.

Around 5¾ miles you pass some more stock ponds and perhaps masses of violet and white blue eyed Mary. At mile 6 you come to a significant sweeping turn in the road. If you want to save a mile of hiking, head cross country down the broad grassy hillside to the south and connect with the road again. Otherwise stay on the road and take the big horseshoe turn in a more gradual downhill fashion. At 6½ miles the ridge trail continues straight but you turn left and down toward Long Canyon again. At 6¾ miles you come to where the cross-country route would connect. Soon after is a very confusing junction due in part to overgrown grassy conditions. Continue downhill on the left fork. Before 7¼ miles arrive at the ten-foot high, round metal tank and complete the loop. From here it's a little less than 2 miles of familiar ground back to the beginning for a 9¼-mile loop.

174

SUGARLOAF RIDGE STATE PARK

In the heart of the North Coast Range

DIRECTIONS: You have four ways to reach Sugarloaf by car from Napa Valley. 1) From Calistoga take Petrified Forest Road to Calistoga Road. Turn left on Highway 12 and left again on Adobe Canyon Road. It's 4 miles to the entrance kiosk. 2) From St. Helena take Spring Mountain Road to Calistoga Road. 3) From Oakville take Oakville Grade, which turns into Dry Creek Road then Trinity Road at the crest. Turn right on Highway 12 to Adobe Canyon Road. 4) From south of Napa take Highway 12 west then north to Adobe Canyon Road.

FEES: Day use: $6/vehicle, camping $15-20/night.
DISTANCE: 8¾-mile loop
GRADE: Strenuous
ELEVATION GAIN: 1,500 feet
BEST TIME: Winter, spring, fall
INFO: Sugarloaf State Park, 707/833-5712
Ferguson Observatory, 707/833-6979

The headwaters of Sonoma Creek held the Wappo Indian village of Wilikos long before the Mexicans arrived. It was a seasonal hunting camp, too cold and wet for the winter months. The Wappo were so successful in resisting the

175

Mexican soldiers that colony attempts at Santa Rosa, Fulton and Petaluma were abandoned. In the late 1830s Wappo population dwindled as American settlers took their land, and epidemic diseases took a heavy toll. In the 1850s the remaining Wappo were forcibly relocated to the Mendocino Indian Reservation.

In early pioneer days, no major trail crossed the southern Mayacmas Mountains between Napa and Sonoma valleys, isolating settlers and slowing development. The first to settle in the flat lands west of Sugarloaf Park was sea captain John Wilson, granted the 19,000-acre *Rancho Los Guilicos* in 1837. In 1858 he sold it to Scottish ship carpenter William Hood, who planted vineyard and built a three-story stone winery on Los Guilicos Creek. Hood Mountain is named for him.

The rugged hills and thin soils around Sugarloaf supported marginal agriculture by 1870. The Luttrell family was first to claim the largest piece of bottom land and raise cattle, grow walnuts and subsistence crops. Later owners manufactured charcoal from oak wood between 1905 and 1910. In this era the Reynolds family built the main ranch house and the main access road through Adobe Canyon, supplanting the Nunn's Canyon road from the south.

In 1920 new owner John Warboys sold this parcel to the State of California. They planned to dam the waters of Sonoma Creek watershed and pipe it to Sonoma State Home at Eldridge near Glen Ellen. Plans were already underway when surrounding landowners raised objections and a water rights dispute arose, suspending construction. After fifteen years the issue was settled when Sonoma State Home built a dam near Eldridge. The state hospital, however, continued use of the site as a Scout camp for patients until World War II. In the 1950s the state leased it to Raffo Brothers Milk Transportation Company for cattle grazing until it became the first parcel included in Sugarloaf Ridge State Park in the early 1960s.

Other properties in the surrounding hills were used for cattle and crops, and increasingly by the 1930s for hunting and weekend outings. The Bear Creek Ranch in the extreme northwest corner of the park was homesteaded by the Hurd family of St. Helena by 1914. It was a marginal operation at best. By the 1930s a Napa County group ran a hunting camp here, their only access a rough fire road off Spring Mountain. By the 1960s a new owner obtained access through the park. The ranch house burned in 1967, purportedly occupied at the time by a large group of hippies. The property was included in the state park by 1972.

Sugarloaf Ridge State Park has grown today to more than 2,700 acres, with twenty-five miles of hiking trails. Fifty primitive camp sites are offered in addition to a group camp that holds a hundred people. The Robert Ferguson Observatory, located near the group camp, is open for public viewing. Ask one of the helpful volunteers about the great Leonid meteor shower of 1833 in which hundreds of thousands of meteorites were observed in one night. It was seen all over North America and was so bright it woke many people from sleep. The Observatory's three telescopes include a specially equipped solar viewer, a fourteen-inch reflector that takes digital photos, and a forty-inch reflector for star gazing.

The park's location in the Coast Range is a transitional one, between the cool, moist coastal air and dry inland air. Several distinct habitats are thus found in close proximity: redwood forest, oak woodland, mixed evergreen forest and chaparral. Wildlife remains abundant, with recent sightings of wild turkey, bobcat, mountain lion and wild pig. Some of the park's best trails are the newest, like the Goodspeed and Brushy Peaks trails.

TRAIL NOTES:

The following loop lets you experience the heart of Sugarloaf Park. From the gentle waters of Sonoma Creek to windy ridgetop views encompassing more than six counties, you'll see nearly all this area has to offer. At a fast clip this trail can be done in a few hours, but to thoroughly enjoy it, allow three-quarters of a day.

Find the trailhead for the Meadow Trail next to an interpretive display at the main parking lot. Immediately there is a connector trail to Bald Mountain Trail — stay right. The meadow on your left often holds grazing deer. To the west is Hood Mountain. This watershed holds two Bald Mountains within two air miles of each other. To the southeast is Bald Mountain (2,275 feet, also called Little Bald Mountain), just outside the park boundary. To the north is the better known Bald Mountain (2,729 feet), the one you will climb today.

Pass through a zone of chaparral and come to an even larger expanse of meadow. At ⅓ mile the Lower Bald Mountain Trail splits left. Bear to the right on the Meadow Trail. Descend to the Group Camp at ½ mile. This site features a horse corral and two stone barbecues with a crossbar spit for roasting meat. An alternate paved route ends here. To your immediate left is Ferguson Observatory. A new feature of the park allows you at this point to begin a "Walk to Pluto." The relative size of our solar system's planets and their relative distance from the sun will be indicated by signs along the path. Thus, you pass Mars in about 300 feet but won't arrive at Pluto until the most distant ridge 3 miles away!

Go past the metal gate across a small creek and onto the dirt road. After winter rains this is a great place to look for animal tracks such as deer and raccoon. An expansive meadow to the right is punctuated by a single enormous coast live oak. As the meadow ends beyond ¾ mile you walk under tall bay and alder along Sonoma Creek. On the left is a bay tree seventy feet high with ten separate trunks up to two feet in diameter.

You'll find a wonderful picnic site at mile 1. Towering over a picnic table by the creek is a maple so large I once, in its dormant stage, mistook it for an oak. Cross the bridge over Sonoma Creek and at 1⅓ miles come to the Gray Pine Trail junction. Stay right on Meadow Trail, soon meeting another junction. Meadow Trail continues along the road as Hillside Trail. You turn left onto Brushy Peaks Trail.

The wide trail now follows the Malm Fork of Sonoma

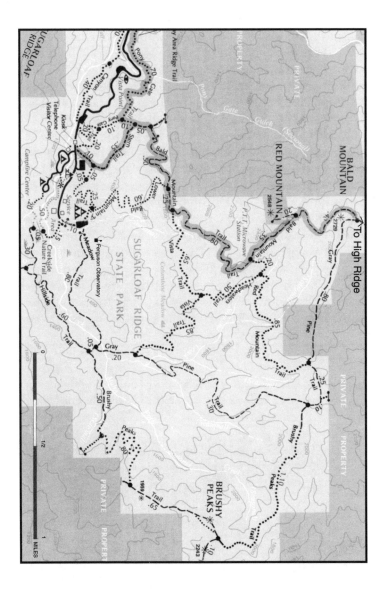

Creek. In late spring or early summer the lovely yellow Mariposa lily brightens the scene. The trail begins a steep climb around 1¾ miles. Behind you appear (Sugarloaf Park's) Bald Mountain and Red Mountain. A fallen madrone blocks an old private road on your right. Stay left here and the trail soon narrows. It switchbacks in big low angle sweeps up a steep hill through mature madrone/Douglas fir forest. Below is the Malm Fork, now a vertiginous drop.

Come out into the sunlight at mile 2 with a view back to where you started. As you approach the headwaters of Malm Fork you have extensive views of the Sonoma/Napa ridge line. Before 2¾ miles you come to the ridge that divides the Sonoma Creek and Dry Creek watersheds. This is a fine destination in itself, with a new picnic table under live oaks. Views all the way down Dry Creek take your eyes to Mount Veeder, the city of Napa and San Pablo Bay.

Turn left as you are now at the south boundary of the park. The terrain changes dramatically to chamise and manzanita and the trail turns into a steep, rocky fire road. Mount St. John (2,375 feet) is to the east. One former owner

Looking across the slopes of Bald Mountain to Mount St. John

was Judge Hastings, who founded Hastings Law School. A large portion is now owned by movie director Francis Ford Coppola. The fire road sweeps up and down in giant roller coaster dips that unfortunately cannot be enjoyed at a hiker's pace. Brushy Peaks is pure chaparral territory with buckbrush, toyon, scrub oak and chamise.

An unmarked junction appears at 3¼ miles. Those wanting more uphill punishment can ascend the steep fire road to top Brushy Peak. Most will want to take the right fork, a level trail through a chaparral tunnel to a trail sign. Both trails lead to the same place. Turn right and come to another junction. To the right a trail leads to Peak 2,243 — you take the not obvious left fork northeast through brush.

Reach the ridgetop at 3¾ miles for the best views of Napa Valley on this trail. The view of St. Helena is particularly good, and many town residents will be able to see their own house with good binoculars. Turn sharply left at a metal stake. Hikers will make good time as they hit the road again, while new plant species like chaparral pea and pearly everlasting appear. At mile 4 the road roller coasters again. Groves of deciduous oaks punctuate the chaparral.

At 4⅝ miles pass under high voltage power lines that march through Napa and Sonoma valleys. Fire has been a stranger here lately, indicated by thick-trunked chamise to six feet tall. The Brushy Peaks Trail ends at 4¾ miles and you continue on the Gray Pine Trail to the right. Soon you pass a private road overly secure with two gates.

Larger black oaks appear along with smaller madrone and bay. At mile 5 you'll see in a window through the trees vineyard-terraced Spring Mountain near St. Helena. A steep hill leads to the Red Mountain Trail junction. Stay on the fire road passing an old manzanita twelve feet tall. In the spring bush lupine will be flowering. After relentless uphill, emerge onto the first meadows that stretch to Bald Mountain. On your right is a superb black oak forest that continues nearly to the mountain top.

The last uphill of the trail ends on the bald flats of Bald

Mountain. Two interpretive displays locate and give mileage to 30 peaks and landmarks in the region, including Pyramid Peak 129 miles east in the Sierra. I talked with a cyclist here who gained the top in 40 minutes from Bald Mountain trailhead. Many bikers loop back via Gray Pine Trail.

The downward-bound trail takes a big sweep around the hilltop, passing the High Ridge Trail which dead-ends after a mile and a half at the old Hurd homestead. The Bald Mountain Trail passes serpentine rock outcrops and erosion gullies until meeting a paved road beyond 6¼ miles. The right fork leads to the microwave towers atop Red Mountain. Go left, passing a picnic table at 6½ miles. The roadside is alive with wildflowers in spring. The Red Mountain Trail veers off left and downhill. To the south you can see the ridge with Brushy Peaks Trail and realize you have circumscribed the entire watershed in a giant crescent.

A bench offers a rest at mile 7. Descend another ⅓ mile to pass spring-fed sword ferns. Just beyond is a lovely vernal pool in an area closed for renovation. On my approach I mistook a tree frog cacophony for bull frogs. They were loud enough to record on my little battery-run Sony from one hundred feet away! Circle the pool and come to the Vista Trail junction. A rest bench at 7¾ miles marks the lower Bald Mountain Trail. This is a good shortcut to the trailhead if you have an appointment to keep.

Continue steeply down the paved road past large bosses of polished green serpentine. There is an interesting blend of chaparral and woodland species past a hairpin turn at mile 8. In ¼ mile pass a gate. Your loop continues as Stern Trail, now gravelled. A road also goes north but soon ends in private property. The Pony Gate Trail junction appears at 8⅜ miles. To your left are massive erosion gullies. Now it's clear why the road was routed away from this chronically unstable slope. Late in the day I was able to photograph a dozen deer grazing as contentedly as cows in these meadows. At a junction you have the choice of heading straight to the road or continuing on trail through meadows to the parking lot at 8¾ miles.

McCORMICK RANCH:
HOMESTEAD TO MAPLE GLEN

DIRECTIONS: From North Main Street in St. Helena, turn left at Madrona Avenue, then right on Spring Mountain Road and cross the mountains into Sonoma County. Turn left on Calistoga Road then left onto Highway 12. Turn left on Los Alamos Road and drive 5 miles to Hood Mountain Regional Park.

DISTANCE: 3¾ miles one way, 7½ miles round trip

GRADE: Strenuous

ELEVATION GAIN: 1000 feet +

BEST TIME: Spring, fall

INFO: Sugarloaf Ridge State Park, 707/833-5712

MAP: Get the Hood Mountain Regional Park Map for trails at McCormick.

DOGS: Not allowed on state park trails, OK in Hood Mountain Park

WARNINGS: Hours are 8 a.m. to sunset. Entrance is blocked by a locked gate at night. There is a restroom but no potable water anywhere in the park.

TRAIL NOTES:

Walk down the paved road that was washed out for many years, repaired, then washed out again. Plans are in the works for rehabilitation. Note the vineyard on a hilltop to the north, it will serve as a good visual guide later for the considerable elevation gain today. You get a nice selection of maples and black oaks alongside the road and an understory plant called coyote brush, a dioeceous plant (either male or female). Sometimes, if you crush a leaf between your fingers it will have a strong lemony smell. Pass the Rasmussen orchard (private) at ⅕ mile. At ⅜ mile is the junction for the Alder Glen Trail, a shortcut you can take to the Hood Mountain-Homestead Meadow Trail. At ½ mile you come to the temporarily inaccessible main parking lot, ranger kiosk with pay phone, picnic tables and display maps and information.

Continue down the hill on switchbacks past more picnic tables until the junction with the Alder Glen Trail on the left, a pleasant side trip along the north fork of Santa Rosa Creek that runs about ¼ mile until connecting again with our trail. Continue on the Homestead Trail through shady forest past a concrete freeway median barrier used creatively here as a retaining wall. You'll soon come to the old Homestead Meadow where you'll find a hand-dug rock-lined well, a gravesite, and the collapsed remains of a building used to separate cream from milk dating from the 1920s. To find them, locate a shallow draw with a walnut tree to its left just before the three-way junction. Follow the draw uphill to another healthier walnut tree where the grasses will be green in summer and the ground probably marshy in winter and spring. The old well is covered by a screen for safety. It held water up to about the ten-foot depth even in a drought year. Now go left and up to the ridgetop where a gravesite has been commemorated by a recently built picket fence. No tombstone remains, but one has an appreciation for the peaceful resting spot afforded these homesteaders. Return to the trail and look for the creamery building at the three-way junction. It's easy to miss, a collapsed heap of wood and metal on a shady knoll left of the picnic tables.

A gruesome historical footnote is worth a digression. In June 1921 a woodcutter and water witcher named Robert Mills lived with his young wife and two small children in this very remote location. For unknown reasons an employee named Reynolds shot and killed both of his employers then turned the gun on himself. The homestead was far from town and isolated by poor roads, and neighbors were only seen every week or two. The children might have been doomed also but for a fortunate synchronicity when a neighbor dropped by that day to return a borrowed rake. The two children, only six months and two years old, were

Looking up at the Grandmother Oak

found safe and adopted by relatives.

Turn left at a three-way junction and shortly come to the McCormick Ranch turnoff. There is one picnic table, then a low water crossing of North Fork Santa Rosa Creek. You can expect foot and bike traffic to diminish drastically as you head into this more remote part of the park.

Enjoy the brief level walk alongside South Fork Santa Rosa Creek because soon the road tilts skywards. This is good, lonely country out here, dense Douglas fir forest on the north facing slopes, oak and buckeye on the south facing slopes. At $1^{1}/_{5}$ miles is the Quercus Trail sign, not really a junction. Climb steeply through sun and shade past Clarkia and Chinese houses in late spring. On the shady north and east slopes are native bunch grasses. Normally associated with riparian habitat, they can grow well here too. Beyond 1½ miles you reach a fine view of the south fork watershed. Come to the Headwaters Trail junction before 2 miles. The lower Headwaters Trail goes right, soon ending at a private property inholding. Go left and uphill through an expansive grassy meadow that features the royal purple harvest brodiaea. Tall grass may hide gopher or rattlesnakes here in late spring. Finally the trail levels off and passes some chaparral before arriving at the Grandmother Oak Trail before 2¼ miles. This reportedly features the largest coast live oak in the world. Continue uphill just a bit more into the open. If you look due west you can see your starting point at the end of Los Alamos Road.

After a brief downhill take a hard right turn (east) and intersect the high tension power towers that cross the Napa-Sonoma county line, White Sulphur Springs watershed, Napa Valley and points east. The Wildcat Trail junction soon appears on the left. That trail deadends at North Fork Santa Rosa Creek, not all that far from the start. If you're adventurous, a loop trail might be possible by finishing down the north fork streambed itself to the Alder Glen Trail.

Now continue on the Maple Glen Trail. You may see the sun yellow Mariposa lily, usually growing singly, but sometimes in great masses. Pass through an old ranch gate at 2½ miles, then through black oak forest. At 2¾ miles pass a hillside seep with a double sink, water catchment basin made of cement.

A lone picnic table in an overgrown meadow just after mile 3 can serve as your private lunch spot. The trail, built by ranchers who preferred riding to walking, gets very steep again at 3⅜ miles. The trail ends at a locked gate at 3¾ miles. For now, visitors must turn back, but someday a trail is planned to connect with the main body of Sugarloaf State Park.

HOOD MOUNTAIN to SUGARLOAF STATE PARK

DIRECTIONS: From Main Street St. Helena turn left at the last signal light north (Madrona) then right on Spring Mountain Road. Go over Spring Mountain then left on Calistoga Road. At Highway 12 turn left. Turn left again on Pythian Road and follow signs 1.3 miles to the trailhead. There you'll find space for 28 cars, a restroom, potable water, bicycle racks and a display board with map and a map dispenser.

FEE: $5

DISTANCE: 7 miles one way

GRADE: Strenuous

ELEVATION GAIN: 2,000 feet

BEST TIME: Spring, fall

DOGS ALLOWED: OK in regional park, not in the State Park

INFO: For Hood Mtn.: Sonoma County Regional Parks 707/565-2041
For Sugarloaf State Park: 707/833-5712

MAP: Get the Hood Mountain Regional Park Map for the best view of this route.

SUGGESTIONS: For the one-way hike you'll need to park a shuttle vehicle at Goodspeed Trailhead on Adobe Canyon Road before main entrance to Sugarloaf Park.

WARNINGS: Although only 7 miles, 4,000 feet elevation gain/loss makes this a big day. Watch for rattlers on the grassy trails, especially in April and May.

Like the lands in and around Sugarloaf State Park, the area we now know as Hood Mountain was in 1839 a Spanish land grant named Rancho Los Guilicos. The California Governor at the time granted the Rancho to Scottish sea captain John Wilson. The ranch of nearly 19,000 acres was used primarily to graze enormous herds of cattle to produce cowhides. Wilson sold his ranch to William Hood in 1858, a man who had made his fortune in the San Francisco building boom following the Gold Rush. Rancho Los Guilicos, believed named after a large Wappo village in the area, Wilikos, continued to prosper as a cattle ranch and later vineyards, fruit orchards and grains increased the productivity. In the following two decades squatters claiming the more remote parts of his ranch as their own became a major concern. His ranch began to dwindle in size until only 1700 acres were left. By 1877 his financial situation necessitated sale of large parcels not yet claimed by squatters.

One of these squatter families was the Hendrickson's. David and Martha Hendrickson and their four children came out west from Minnesota to settle on what is now known as the Orchard Meadow at the junction of the Upper and Lower Johnson Trails. Under the Homestead Act of 1862 they were required to live there for at least five years and make significant improvements to the value of the property, after which they were granted ownership in January 1891. The Hendrickson's planted walnuts, peach, apple and olive trees, cultivated an acre of potatoes each year and raised hogs, chickens and milk cows.

On high ground to the east of the meadow they built several structures, three of which are standing as of 2007. The first structure, believed to be built in 1875, was the main house, a two story, single room affair with a loft and outside porch. The cooking was done in a wood-burning stove inside the fireplace (the chimney vent hole for the woodstove is easily seen). At the back of the house a ramp led outside to a path that led to three small cabins used as sleeping quarters by the family and hired hands. Two of these sleeping quarters are still standing. A third standing structure in between the two cabins is the bathhouse. There was also a root cellar, still more or less intact, a barn, and cream separator for butter production, now gone or down to foundations only. Quite visible from the hiking trail today are four wooden posts known as wickets and in combination with fencing kept animals out but allowed people to pass by means of a gate. The Hendrickson's built a cistern to capture water from a spring just up trail from the homestead.

The Hendrickson children attended school in Santa Rosa, likely boarding in town for the week due to the isolated location and returning on weekends. After pioneering here for thirty years David and Martha sold the place and retired to Santa Rosa. It would change hands many times over the next century. The next owner was John Minges of Arkansas, a miner, who developed the hillside behind the homestead into a quicksilver mine. Those scars have been hidden by vegetative growth, and evidence of mining is not obvious, at least from the perspective of Orchard Meadow. That period lasted only five years. We can surmise it was not a highly profitable venture.

Between 1909 and 1918 U.S. Senator Thomas Kearns was owner of the homestead, adjacent lands and Hood Mansion, his summer home. It was here that he entertained President Theodore Roosevelt. A mining entrepreneur from Utah, he increased the size of the ranch to 1700 acres. Subsequent owners reversed this trend by parceling off much of the ranch lands. In 1924 a fraternal organization called the Knights of Pythias bought the remaining hundred plus acres and used Hood Mansion to house orphaned children and the aged. They used the homestead site for overnight retreats.

The Knights succumbed to financial problems and sold to A.B. Knowles, another entrepreneur. He leased the homestead site to hunting clubs and built his own ranch house. In 1957 another San Francisco businessman Willard Johnson and his wife Alice bought 460 acres including the ranch house, renaming it the Panorama Ranch for its views of the Valley of the Moon. The Johnsons had two children, Elizabeth and Willard Jr., the latter inheriting the property in 1987. Two trails in the park are named for the Johnson family.

Sonoma County Regional Parks and Open Space District purchased the property in 2003 and incorporated the 335-acre Panorama Ranch into Hood Mountain Regional Park, creating trails, picnic sites and interpretive displays. This purchase is part of a very welcome trend occurring throughout the North Bay and elsewhere. It counteracts the trend toward parcelization of the last 100 years. These lands have come full circle and can now return to the more or less natural state they enjoyed under the care of indigenous tribes.

TRAIL NOTES:

Start the trail on either side of the parking lot. The trail does some gymnastics to accommodate right of way issues with private landowners. Several of the homes you pass belong or belonged to the Johnson family. Stretch your hamstrings for .3 mile on a very steep paved section of road. Beautiful mixed evergreen forest of maple, Douglas fir, bay and live oak protect a steep slope leading to Hood Mountain Creek below. After ⅓ mile veer right following signs around a final residence as the road turns to gravel. Turn off left very quickly onto trail. In June a 'weed' called mullein with large woolly green leaves and a spike of yellow flowers grows six feet high. Before ½ circle around three redwood water tanks. The main supply pipe for these tanks, once propped into the crotch of an oak, is now completely encircled by the trunk.

The trail crosses a private road at a farm gate and parallels the road briefly. Get back on the road, cross the creek, and climb a short uphill stretch. After ⅔ mile look closely for the trail turnoff to the right — the trail sign is on the opposite side of the road and could be missed. Easier trail leads through open Douglas fir forest high above the creek. Note that some trees have been cut to stump. Some selective logging was done by the Johnsons prior to sale. Also, some trees were cut during trail construction and some are afflicted with fire blight.

At mile 1 is the Panorama Trail junction. A longer option turns right on Pond Trail, also leading to Orchard Meadow. Our trail takes the left fork with pleasant uphill walking. Hood Mountain is still wild and big enough to provide habitat for black bear. Though it's unlikely to see the nocturnal Ursa, large scat mixed with berries ('bearies') is a strong indicator of their presence. At 1⅓ miles is a large meadow, the largest freshwater wetland in the park. A new-looking circular concrete water tank holds clear spring water from one of many sources in this area. Through a complex water system including ponds and piping, it will eventually end up at the lower parking lot. In the meadow are a dozen or so walnut trees from the 1870s.

Come to the junction of the Pond Trail and a new display case with map of Hood Mountain Regional Park and Sugarloaf State Park. This is the end of the Lower Johnson Trail and the beginning of the Upper Johnson Trail. Just beyond is the Hendrickson homestead with its three one-room cabins still standing, and the main house ruins with only a chimney intact. This area is archaeologically sensitive, please respect the signs and fencing and stay out. At the upper end of the site is an area allowing close viewing and good photos of these picturesque, tilting relics.

Continue up steeply to the Knight's Retreat Trail junction at 1⅔ miles. A short detour affords a view of Orchard Meadow from a knoll. The Upper Johnson Trail takes six steep but well graded switchbacks through mixed evergreen forest to the ridgetop. Note the rock armoring at every creek and rivulet crossing. A lot of work went into this trail. As the forest thins wild rose appears, then some chaparral, Douglas fir segues to cypress and knobcone pine. Shortly you arrive at a top at 2¼ miles. Sonoma Valley is seen to the west and upper Napa Valley to the east including Mount St. Helena and the Palisades/Wildlake Ridge.

It's another ⅞ mile to the summit. Leave the road at the summit trail sign. Ignore the tempting use trail that bolts straight for the ridge where a double arrow indicates the real trail. Climb through madrone, and tanbark oak forest to near the top, where a bay, an oak and a madrone all grow together in a fine horizontal mélange. Reach the summit at 3⅛ miles, a trampled patch of dirt without views, a clearly disappointing and anticlimactic moment for all your effort. It can, however, host the spectacular purple pentstemon in May.

The downhill portion of the day starts with a narrow, eroded gully past an overhanging rock ledge. At 3⅜ miles is the turnoff to Gunsight Rock. It's another ⅜ mile out to this spectacular lunch spot with stupendous views of Sonoma Valley. Take the Nattkemper Trail left. Even if you've missed the views from the Gunsight the main trail affords its own awesome view of the Highway 12 corridor from a high meadow left of the Gunsight. Traverse through oak woodland. An old manzanita past 3⅝ miles has a trunk one and a half feet in diameter. A short steep set of switchbacks leads to a steeply inclined meadow with fine old specimen trees. Be cautious on this steep and rocky portion. It offers fine wildflower viewing in spring.

At 4⅛ miles we spotted a natural tree 'swing' next to a massive bay tree with odd burls and stopped to rest. As I rose to leave there was a frantic scrabbling in the tree above, then a large alligator lizard smacked down where my face had been a moment before. He lay stunned and unmoving but quite alive for several minutes until we gently moved him off trail. Alligator lizards usually seen on terra firma, will climb trees, and more rarely, fall out of them.

As you come to steep grassy meadows sweeping down to valley and canyon, reach a fine rest bench at 4¼ miles. Dedicated to Clark Nattkemper, a teacher, backpacker and conservationist, this was his favorite place on the mountain—mine too. If you're coming from Sugarloaf and Gunsight Rock is too far,

Looking south toward Bald Mountain from the Nattkemper Trail

this makes a fine high point. This leg of trail, known formerly as the Goodspeed, was renamed in Clark's honor. Just down the trail pass a display case with a poetic tribute to him.

Continue past a lone bay tree surrounded by vast, sweeping meadows, a classic photo op. Round a bend to see Sugarloaf's Bald Mountain, passing golden fairy lantern and checker mallow in spring. Before 5 miles the trail turns rough and rocky — continue relentlessly down. Reach the bottom around 5⅞ miles and ford a stream on slick serpentine rock. Climb through oak woodlands via switchbacks. In late spring Indian pinks may brighten your way.

At 6 miles the Nattkemper Trail ends. Cross a private road and continue ascending the Goodspeed Trail. Spring 2007 saw a month long closure for trail renovation here, with completion of phase II due in spring 2008. From the ridgetop, your trail descends in a series of broad, sweeping and technically perfect switchbacks through chaparral slopes until bottoming out by shady Bear Creek. Cross a couple of wooden footbridges for an easy finish in lush riparian habitat before reaching Adobe Canyon Road at 7 miles.

BLUE RIDGE

Eastern edge of the North Coast Range

DIRECTIONS: From Napa take Highway 12 to Interstate 80, then I-505 to Winters, or from Rutherford take Highway 128 to Winters. Continue north on I-505 for 10 miles, then turn west on Highway 16. Drive 30 miles through rural Capay Valley to *lower* Yolo County Park.

An alternate scenic route goes north on Highway 29 to Lower Lake, then continues on Highway 53 to its end. Turn right and follow Highway 20 east, then Highway 16 south 10 miles to *lower* Yolo County Park.

After turning off the highway, veer left. If the gate is closed in winter, park nearby. If open, continue on County Road 40 (Rayhouse Road) then head down to the creek, cross the low-water concrete bridge and park in a small lot at the first junction. Now on foot, turn off Road 40 onto an access road that leads to group camping. The north trailhead starts at the Ada Merhoff stone memorial next to two BLM trail markers.

DISTANCE: 8½ miles one way

GRADE: Strenuous

ELEVATION GAIN: 2,000+ feet

BEST TIME: Spring

DOGS ALLOWED: On leash

INFO: Bureau of Land Management, 707/468-4000

SUGGESTIONS: Many hikers will find attaining the ridge a satisfying destination. From the top at mile 3 a volunteer trail leads to a spectacular overlook. Continuing on the main trail another mile takes you to Peak 2,868.

The round trip of nearly 17 miles can be done in a long day. The best way, though, is to hike it one way from south to north. If County Road 40 is open, car pool or have someone drop you at Fiske Creek Trailhead. That way you avoid the 2,000-foot gain at the start.

Blue Ridge was named for the bluish cast of the blue oaks and chaparral on its west slope. These mountains were Patwin Indian territory, a non-agrarian tribe of traders whose routes followed Putah and Cache creeks to the coastal valleys and the sea. Trapper Ewing Young camped in Capay Valley in 1832 (Kaipai means "stream" in Patwin). He named the stream Cache Creek for the cache of goods his party stored here. The very next year flooding in the Central Valley created a malaria epidemic that killed three quarters of the Patwin nation.

The Patwins' troubles increased in 1836 when an alliance was formed between Commander Vallejo of the Sonoma garrison and Solano, the powerful Suisun chief. Solano agreed not to molest Mexican settlers in Sonoma and Napa in exchange for help in subduing his enemies, the Patwins. Later the few Patwin survivors were relocated to rancherias. One still exists in Capay Valley.

A few large ranchos were formed in the 1840s, notably by Demesio, Santiago and Francisco Berryessa in upper Capay Valley, and by naturalized citizen William Gordon. The Gordon Ranch was a well-known and popular rendezvous for settlers and hunters. It was the site of a stopover for the Bear Flag Party coming from John C.

Fremont's Feather River camp in June 1846. They recruited another member and continued on through Tully Canyon to Berryessa, Pope and Napa valleys, eventually capturing the Sonoma garrison and declaring California a republic on June 14, 1846.

The 1850s saw general settlement of Capay Valley. The mountains, though, were rugged and saw sparse development. Charles F. Reed, a West Point civil engineer who earlier surveyed the town of Knight's Landing, opened a quicksilver mine near Little Blue Ridge on Davis Creek in the 1860s. The railroad pushed as far as the hamlet of Rumsey in upper Capay Valley by 1888, but fond plans of extending it through Cache Creek canyon to Lake County never materialized.

In 1906 on Cache Creek occurred one of the greatest land slides in California history, but its significance was lost due to the 8.25 magnitude earthquake that struck San Francisco only thirteen days earlier. The slide happened on May 1, 1906, near Trout Creek, a tributary of Cache Creek. Residents downstream in Capay Valley noticed the creek level had dropped five feet overnight, but the slide area was so inaccessible that it was two days before the cause could be confirmed. The slide that completely blocked Cache Creek was one hundred feet high and 500 feet wide on top, impounding 12,000 acre-feet of water in a lake four miles long.

Mariposa lily

Residents in

Capay Valley evacuated and camped in the hills. They waited five days until the creek broke the dam, when the flood with its debris devastated the town of Rumsey. No one was killed or injured. The San Francisco disaster overshadowed this event, which quickly faded into obscurity. Geologists today say that the quake (plus heavy rainfall that winter) could easily have been a factor in the slide. The highly fractured and jointed mudstones, shales, conglomerates and sandstones in Cache Creek Canyon will continue to produce large and small landslides in the future.

Capay Valley's orchards and open fields today make it an agricultural oasis that is unfortunately starting to feel the taint of urban encroachment. Since the advent of the automobile, Cache Creek Canyon has been a popular motor outing in the spring when hundreds of native western redbud trees are in bloom. Campers, fishers, hunters and white water rafters frequent this area too. Since the mid-1980s and the creation of the Blue Ridge Trail, hiking has become more popular. The Bureau of Land Management has been actively improving the trail for several years. Its best features are its remoteness, abundant wildlife and spring wildflowers, and outstanding views.

TRAIL NOTES:

Blue Ridge Trail has three distinct personalities. The first 2 steep miles of trail are the prettiest, partially shaded by mixed evergreen forest and highlighted with many wildflowers. The third mile, definitely the toughest of the trip, is even steeper, with poor footing, many switchbacks and prone to overgrowth. With most of the climbing over, the last 5½ miles of trail is an unending swath through monotonous chaparral, saved by superb 360 degree views and decorated to the end with wildflowers in spring.

The trail shows you its teeth from the start, climbing steeply through a mix of oak, buckeye and gray pine, with a stunning display of wildflowers like paintbrush, brodiaea, mariposa lily and golden fairy lantern. Before ¼ mile the trail really starts to climb, following a small creek. On Glasscock Mountain to the north, entire hillsides of chamise will be a riot of bloom in May.

At ½ mile pass under a buckeye tree, cross the creek and traverse the opposite hillside with the first major views of Cache Creek Canyon to the northwest. Another sharp turn at ¾ mile brings you face to face with your main challenge, the prominent 2,000 foot uplift seen from the highway. Un-

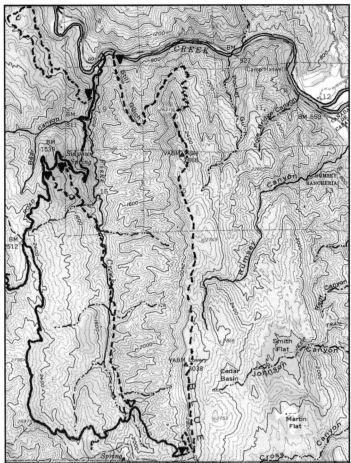

Blue Ridge

maintained, this trail would be a poison oak gauntlet.

Cross a creek scoured wide by the 1995 floods at 1¼ miles and make your only foray of the hike into grassland. The trail turns unreasonably steep at 1½ miles. Look for the white blooms of prickly poppies in late May.

Around mile 2 you climb from north-facing wooded hillsides to east-facing brushy slopes with views of upper Capay Valley. The uniform chamise is interrupted only by occasional ceanothus, gray pine, chaparral pea or monkeyflower. The next mile would be gruesome on a hot summer day. Keep an eye out for ticks, including the tiny lyme disease-carrying, red-bodied *Ixodes pacifica*.

Near the ridgetop at 3 miles is an unmarked junction. The right fork is a volunteer trail leading shortly to a view straight down the great uplift you have climbed. If the Central Valley is clear you'll see the Sierra Nevada Range east of it. To the west are Little Blue Ridge, Cobb Mountain, and a little south of that, Mount St. Helena. Take the left fork to continue on Blue Ridge.

A gradual climb leads to Peak 2,868, also called Fiske

Peak, at mile 4, where you can sign the summit register enclosed in a tin can. Follow a vague path along the ridge, where Indian paintbrush grows in spring, until the trail turns obvious in the chaparral. The path is fairly level and open through miles 5 and 6. Occasional fire rings on the trail itself show the limited camping possibilities. After Lower Capay Valley comes into view, descend to a notch in the ridge at the head of Rumsey Canyon as you near mile 7. The scent of myriad blue blossom California lilac in the spring makes this location a wild garden.

Begin the ascent to Peak 3,038, Lowery Peak. The summit bench mark is off the main trail. You may notice a low profile green dome to the east — this is a water source for wildlife placed by BLM. To the west is Rayhouse Road (Road 40) a seasonal road that leads to Lake County. The trail abruptly abandons the ridge and heads steeply down to reach Fiske Creek Trailhead at 8½ miles.

FROG POND TRAIL

DIRECTIONS: From Napa Valley you have two options, which merge at Middletown. Take Highway 29 north from Calistoga 16 miles over Mount St. Helena to Middletown, or take Deer Park Road one mile north of St. Helena to Angwin, then Howell Mountain Road north to Pope Valley. Turn left and proceed through Pope Valley and Butts Canyon to Middletown. Take Highway 29 to Lower Lake, turn right on Highway 53, continuing north to Highway 20. Turn right and follow Highway 20 to Highway 16 just past the Bear Valley turnoff. Turn right on Highway 16 and follow it to Lower Yolo County Campground. If the low water bridge is closed for the season, park in a turnout near the gate. If the gate is open, drive 0.5 mile across the bridge, past a stone barn and stone house and up the road to the signed Frog Pond Trailhead on your right.

BEST TIME	Spring
INFO:	Bureau of Land Management, Ukiah, 707/468-4000. YoloHiker website: yolohiker.org
DISTANCE:	5 miles round trip from the gate
GRADE:	Moderate, elevation gain 660 feet
DOGS ALLOWED:	On leash
SUGGESTIONS:	Avoid this hike in summer because it would be a cooker.

TRAIL NOTES:

If you park at the gate, head downhill for almost ¼ mile and cross the bridge. This is fun to do because there are no railings and you're practically on the water. Pass the turnoff to Blue Ridge Trail on the left, then pass a bridge over Fiske Creek. Now pass a new looking, picturesque stone barn and stone house. Just before ½ mile come to the Frog Pond Trailhead, signed "five-mile loop" (not accurate from this point). Ascend past parking for a few cars, then veer right and go through a gate where the road soon narrows to trail. On our hike in late April the center of the trail held masses of the delicate, dandelion-like flower called microseris. To the north and east Mount Glasscock and Mount Fiske straddle Cache Creek like sentinels.

Pass through open forest of gray pine, black oak and blue oak. After the first climb, the trail traverses the hillside well above Cache Creek. In spring you may see Chinese houses and twining snake lily, named for its stem up to five feet long. At one mile you saunter through one of the several pleasing blue oak woodlands on this loop trail. Before 1¼ miles you come to two trail junctions. The first junction may be taken either way — the left fork is a small shortcut, the right slightly longer but preferable because it takes you to a fine overlook of Cache Creek and Lower Yolo County Campground, where the waving wands of western wallflower dance on the cliff edge in spring. The second junction is the start of the loop. It may be taken left or right. We go right.

At 1½ miles water seepage makes for lush growth of ceanothus and other vegetation, attracting many birds. Wind your way among blue-eyed grass and blue oaks as you climb steeply. Round a ridge and crest out at two trail arrow signs at 1¾ miles. To the south and east is a sea of chaparral, with an amazingly sharp demarcation line between it and the oak woodland. Head into this sea of chamise and buckthorn with impressive stands of yerba santa up to eight feet high.

Soon you come to a key junction. Two signs point left, but if you want to see the Frog Pond, take a short detour to the right. In a low rain year you might not see much. When we saw it the pond was a sickly greenish color with no shade on the banks. However, it is favorite habitat of the raucous bull frog. Continue through the chaparral 'high seas,' except at 2 miles you come to more lush vegetation beside a creek. Fiske Peak and Blue Ridge are prominent.

Before 2¼ miles the trail does some strange things as it seems to wander aimlessly, as if lost, nearly doubling back

Looking down at Cache Creek from the Frog Pond Trail

on itself at one point, before straightening out and heading more logically for a blue oak meadow on a ridge. Pass a land slump scarp in the meadow at 2¾ miles. If you wander around this country enough, such slumps are a common sight. The blue oak meadow offers a good place for lunch. Now head mostly downhill, traversing through perhaps the finest blue oak woodland of the hike, very attractive hill country. The trail descends steeply until the loop's end. Turn right to see the shortcut you bypassed on the way up, then follow familiar trail back to the start.

FISKE CREEK TRAIL

DIRECTIONS: Same as for Blue Ridge until across the low water bridge. Then continue 2.5 miles up Rayhouse Road to the Fiske Creek Trailhead on the left. Parking is limited.

DISTANCE: 3¾ miles one way. You may return the same way or have a car shuttle (4WD required).

GRADE: Easy

ELEVATION GAIN: 300 feet+/ 300 feet-

BEST TIME: Spring

DOGS ALLOWED: On leash

INFO: BLM, Ukiah, 707/468-4000

TRAIL NOTES:

Pass over a low bar left of the gate and immediately come to great views of Blue Ridge to the east. For the next ¾ mile you descend gently through blue oak woodlands and grasslands. Around ⅓ mile the track may be overgrown but still easy to find. Look for the amazing twining snake lily in late spring, crawling over other plants with its long (2-5 feet) twisting stem which ends in a showy umbel of pink flowers. Beyond ¾ mile the trail dives steeply toward Fiske Creek until leveling out at one mile with the surrounding chaparral showing evidence of the 39,000-acre Rumsey fire of 2004. Take a small leap across an eroded stream gully and reach Fiske Creek at 1¼ miles. You'll usually find some water here even in summer. This is a cool spot to rest, especially on the way back before the uphill finish. You'll see water striders hydroplaning in the pools in search of morsels and perhaps wild grape in flower or fruit on the banks.

Here's an interesting historical side note — the road you're walking on was bulldozed by an owner in the 1980s for the purpose of hauling out rock that was sold for landscaping. Unfortunately, he was doing it illegally and the federal government filed a successful lawsuit. A settlement was reached and the land ended up as the property of the Bureau of Land Management for all of us to enjoy today and tomorrow.

Now the trail more or less follows the creek, crossing it about seven times. A diverse and fascinating variety of plants grow along Fiske Creek as you pass through various plant communities like oak woodland, chaparral, grassy meadows and riparian habitat. Watch for overgrowth sprays of poison oak along the trail and its close cousin, Rhus trilobata or squaw bush, that is not toxic. The overlapping of these plant communities means that animals are frequent. On our hike we saw wild turkey, vultures, red-tailed hawks, heard acorn woodpeckers, and saw bear scat, although seeing a bear would be unusual.

Around 2⅓ miles are a couple of creek crossings marked by trail ducks or cairns. In a high water year it will be a wet crossing. A three-foot diameter blue oak is seen in a meadow at 2¾ mile. At 3 miles we saw extensive displays of mule ears (Wyethia). Go through a tunnel of ceanothus with red columbine hiding in its shade. The canyon continues to narrow, then at 3⅔ miles make the last stream crossing. Step over a low metal bar, and at 3¾ miles the trail contacts Fiske Creek Road. If you walk up the road a little ways and take the first right fork, a picnic table makes a pretty good lunch site.

BALDY MOUNTAIN

This seldom-visited area offers solitude

DIRECTIONS: From Calistoga take Highway 29 to the town of Lower Lake, then take Highway 53 to Highway 20 and turn east. Go north at the junction of Bear Valley Road (Wilbur Springs turnoff) to the north end of Bear Valley. Turn left (west) on Brim Road (Bartlett Springs) and go 2.7 miles to the Walker Ridge Road junction. It's another 2.8 miles to the trailhead at the northeast corner of Indian Valley Reservoir. Look for a Bureau of Land Management (BLM) marker with the hiker symbol. The trail starts at a second BLM marker on the side road.

An alternate road for sturdy vehicles is Walker Ridge Road off Highway 20. It is 15.5 miles from Highway 20 to Bartlett Springs Road.

From the Central Valley, take Interstate 5 to Williams, turn west on Highway 20 to Bear Valley Road.

DISTANCE: 4¼ miles one way

GRADE: Strenuous

ELEVATION GAIN: 1,900 feet

BEST TIME: Winter, spring only. Summer will likely be blazing hot and dry.

DOGS ALLOWED: On leash

INFO: Bureau of Land Management, 707/468-4000

WARNINGS: Be aware this is not the easiest trail to follow. It is indistinct and confusing in places and you may get derailed temporarily. Don't worry. Remember two things: You *will* get to the top eventually *and* your route-finding skills will be finely honed in the process.

SUGGESTIONS: Indian Valley Brodiaea A.C.E.C. (Area of Critical Environmental Concern) holds the entire distribution of this wildflower species. Bear Valley offers one of California's finest wildflower displays in spring.

Great numbers of American Indians called Patwin lived in the valley west of Baldy Mountain, and it came to be known simply as Indian Valley. The Patwin are the southernmost tribe of the Wintun linguistic group, who influenced greatly the Kuksu religion, a spirit-impersonating belief system in which initiates were formally indoctrinated. Many Patwin people were lured to the mission at Sonoma in 1823.

Settlement of Indian Valley by whites was slow. Poor soil overlain by stream-borne gravel deposits made agriculture a marginal business. By 1870 people like Frank Kowalski, Thomas Zimory, John Wilson, Henry Catenburg and Joseph Byron Stanton ran cattle and tried to grow fruit and nut trees. Although many of them had moved on by 1910, they left their names to the canyons, creeks and glades of the region.

Over to the east of Baldy Mountain, Brutus Epperson of Bear Valley saw a business opportunity. Hot springs like Bartlett Springs were doing well, but the only access was from Clear Lake. He formed the Bartlett Springs and Bear Valley Toll Road Company in 1873 to bring visitors from the Central Valley. Chinese built the road in only four months, and that first summer stages carried 600 passengers from Colusa, via the Leesville Road through Bear Valley (where the toll station was), over Baldy Mountain into Indian Valley and on to Bartlett Springs.

Those anxious to avoid the toll soon built the Brim Grade Road through Complexion Canyon (the present road). Epperson, anxious to collect toll, relocated his toll station several times before settling at Barkerville at the northwest corner of Indian Valley. The proprietor, Ephraim Barker, and his wife formed a town of their own by siring twenty-two children, nineteen of whom lived on the ranch. A school was opened in Indian Valley in 1884 but falling population closed it in 1894. Two years later, Epperson's toll road went public when he sold it to the county.

The possibility of a dam in Indian Valley had been discussed as early as 1915. Yolo County farming interests were successful in completing the earthen dam on the North Fork of Cache Creek by 1974. The six-mile-long lake is used mainly for irrigation water, but also for fishing, boating and swimming. There is a small resort on the south end. Blue Oak, Wintun and Barrel Springs camps, primitive sites found on or near Walker Ridge Road east of the lake, are free.

Baldy Mountain Trail was first built by the Department of Fish and Game as a hunter access trail, then fell into disuse. Recently BLM improved it and now it is used occasionally by adventuresome hikers.

TRAIL NOTES:

The rocky trail starts straight uphill. The surrounding plant community is dominated by just a few species: cypress, manzanita, leather oak and gray pine. After ⅓ mile you top the first hill. Your objective, Baldy Mountain, is seen to the southeast. Indian Valley Reservoir stretches to the south, its many drowned trees looking like a graveyard.

Soon you'll descend into a pretty creek canyon. You approach the bottom of the hill at ⅔ mile as the trail takes two switchbacks. The second one is easy to miss. Take a sharp right-angle turn at a good size gray pine and head southeast to the creek. At ¾ mile the trail crosses the creek bed near the confluence of two streams. At the exact confluence a cypress tree separates the two streams. In February the tree will be in bloom. At a touch, pollen will fly off in a delicate yellow cloud that means suffering for the hay fever prone. In June when the creek is going dry, the leopard lily can be a surprising discovery in this hot country. After crossing, find the trail on the right side of a small clearing.

Cross two creeklets and top out at 1 mile. Traverse the shoulder of the second hilltop. Gray pine, cypress and manzanita are still dominant. Look for occasional lines of stones marking the path edge.

An unsigned trail junction at 1¼ miles is now easier to discern — just follow the prominent curving line of rocks uphill. For the next ½ mile the path will be vague at times. In general head south, paralleling the lake.

At 1¾ miles look for a rock cairn as you start to drop into the next canyon. Soon the trail turns east to parallel the creek. At the creek bed crossing is a single silktassel bush. Go steeply uphill and directly away from the lake (east).

Let occasional rock cairns and trail periphery stones guide you in the vicinity of mile 2. Many summits will start

Early hot springs resorts

Several hot springs resorts such as Hough Springs and Allen Springs, located on the Bear Valley-Bartlett Springs road thrived in the 1880s and 1890s. Bartlett Springs, though, was in a class by itself, and became a world famous destination. In 1870 Napa resident Greene Bartlett was near death, legend says, when he was effected a miraculous cure by drinking these waters. It was soon a rustic resort for the seriously ill. In 1877 business partner Sam McMahon began to attract recreational visitors. A toll road was built from Nice/Lucerne on Clear Lake, while a steamer service brought visitors across the lake from Lakeport.

By 1894 Bartlett Springs was called one of the finest natural sanitariums in the world. Five hotels accommodated up to 1,000 guests, attended by 250 employees. A small city

to become visible now. Cobb Mountain and Mount Hannah in southern Lake County, then the volcano of Mount Konocti come into view. Soon after, the higher summits of Saint John Mountain (6,743 feet) and Snow Mountain (7,056 feet) appear to the northwest. On a clear winter day the snow-white summits of Mount Lassen and Mount Shasta provide a startling contrast to the dry, brushy foreground.

You come to the top of a third hill beyond 2¼ miles. At a confusing section, traverse down and left to a pronounced notch. Here is a remarkable change in vegetation. In a single step you finally leave the gray pine-manzanita community and walk into almost solid chamise. The sudden transition is effective for several hundred yards in either direction.

From the notch, climb again through dense, head-high chamise and some scrub oak and buckbrush. Look for exposures of rock called pencil slate, splintered into thousands of fragments, some only one-eighth inch wide.

You are now embarking on perhaps the most frustrating part of the trail. At many of the switchback turns it will be unclear which way to go. Explore options to find the right

built up around it. For entertainment guests were provided a casino, bowling alley, ballroom, concert hall, tennis courts, golf, shuffleboard, croquet, billiards, horseback riding, swimming and, later, hiking trails. Bartlett had its own post office, Wells Fargo office, meat market and general merchandise store. The centerpiece was an open air pavilion built over the original springs. Bartlett Springs attracted the wealthy, the famous, senators, congressmen, governors and once the Queen of Rumania. It was used as a training camp by boxer "Gentleman Jim" Corbett, preparing for his big fight with John L. Sullivan.

Fire destroyed the county landmark in 1934. The open air pavilion survived, and water was still bottled, but the resort was never rebuilt. In the 1980s Vittel of France bought the resort, but despite a major marketing campaign and plans to rebuild, the enterprise failed.

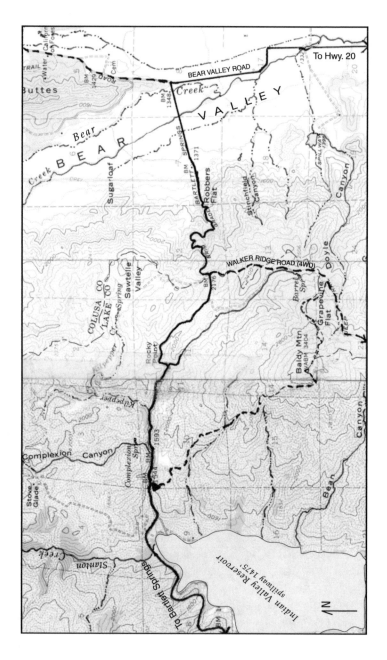

Baldy Mountain's straight-line vegetation change

one. If you find yourself lost in the chaparral, sliding off a thirty degree hillside into sharp-thorned buckbrush, as I did, STOP! Don't panic. Cuss a little, then calmly retrace your steps to the last spot you know was a real trail. Most likely, a turn in the trail was missed. Blue plastic flagging may make this section easier.

Around 2¾ miles the trail stops switchbacking and heads directly to the top of a knoll. From here you can see East Park Reservoir near Stonyford as well as Mount St. Helena to the south. Continue along the poorly cut ridge trail.

The terrain soon changes to cypress forest as you approach the north shoulder of Baldy Mountain at 3¼ miles. From here views east should be excellent on clear days, with nothing between you and the Sierra Nevada.

As well defined trail ascends gradually, the next ½ mile becomes a delight. A knobcone pine forest, with trees to thirty-five feet high, is a pleasure to walk through. This north-facing hillside holds more moisture, evident in the appearance of bay and the size of the oak leaves.

Evergreen oaks appear as the knobcone forest thins. At 3¾ miles you leave the protection of the forest and

211

enter chaparral habitat showing burn scars. Indian Valley Reservoir is now much farther below than when last seen. Come around the shoulder of the last hill at mile 4, with the summit within easy reach. You may see high-flying geese returning to wetlands in the Central Valley. If there is tule fog in the valley, they must use their own brand of radar to find their destination.

At 4¼ miles you reach the somewhat anticlimactic top of Baldy Mountain. A hollow pipe in the ground surrounded by rocks marks the 3,409-foot summit. Just beyond is the first trail marker since the start and a fire road that descends to Walker Ridge Road. If you like, follow the fire road briefly to the south peak for a better lunch site. The eastward view takes in Bear Valley, the Sutter Buttes in the Sacramento Valley, and the Sierra Nevada.

CACHE CREEK
WILDERNESS AREA

Tule elk, eagles and wildflowers

Archaeological evidence indicates that Native Americans occupied the areas now known as Baton Flat, Wilson Valley, and the North Fork of Cache Creek in the vicinity of today's Highway 20 for at least 12,000 years. Extensive oak woodlands and the Cache Creek riparian corridor provided abundant wildlife such as otter, beaver, deer, quail, bear and eagle for the Hill Patwin who called this area home. Modern descendants of these people continue to perform traditional activities here.

The first Euro-American visitors in this region came by 1854 but it wasn't until the 1870s that any settlers put down roots. By 1882 Daniel Hanson had settled on the North Fork of Cache Creek. He owned most of the land from today's Highway 20 bridge to Baton Flat. With his wife he operated the Cache Creek Tavern, a stopover for those traveling between Lakeport and Sacramento. It was in the two story hotel that the post office of Nita (named for one of his daughters) was established in 1893. Typical of those times, it was discontinued only five years later.

Baton Flat is a pocket valley one mile south of the Redbud Trailhead. In 1885 Daniel Hanson sold two parcels here, one to Harvey Bonham and one to William Baton. The Bonhams moved on by 1890. William (Billy) Baton's wife was

213

the school mistress at nearby Grizzley Creek school, until it was moved to Baton Flat. When she died, Billy returned to his native England. All that remain now are some black walnut trees and a flume that carried irrigation water from the main stem of Cache Creek. At one time a single cable tramway with a cable car located at the southeastern tip of the flat enabled crossings at high water.

Before Baton Flat was settled, John Wilson and his son were homesteading a secluded valley several miles downstream. They farmed the richer land and grazed cattle on the rest. The Wilsons had moved on by 1885 leaving Wilson Valley to neighbor James Brenard. He and his wife were still there in April 1906 when one of the largest landslides in California history occurred at Crack Canyon 1½ miles downstream of Wilson Valley (see Blue Ridge chapter). A lake filled up behind the dam for five days, flooding Wilson Valley and backing up as far as the confluence of the north fork and the main stem of Cache Creek. It was deep enough to cover all but the top of James Brenard's house. When the dam broke downstream, all the buildings in the valley were swept away. He rebuilt and stayed until 1911.

Wilson Valley continued to be cultivated by farmers into the 1940s with produce supplied to workers in nearby mercury mines. In 1969 the California Department of Water Resources conducted a study to evaluate the potential for damsites in Wilson Valley, Kennedy Flats and at Blue Ridge, eight miles downstream from Crack Canyon. They concluded that all sites were inappropriate as the probability of further landslides like the one in 1906 was high.

Thus, instead of the inundation of Cache Creek Canyon under 450 feet of water, cattle grazing was the main activity until 1985 when the Bureau of Land Management took ownership. The remaining buildings, in bad condition and a liability, were torn down in the late 1980s. Today the BLM continues its outstanding work toward providing access to the Cache Creek Wilderness Area, designated by congress in 2006. This underused wilderness has great potential for equestrians, hikers, backpackers, river rafters, hunters, bird watchers, photographers, fishers and wildlife enthusiasts.

REDBUD TRAIL

DIRECTIONS: From Napa Valley, take Highway 29 north past Mount St. Helena and Middletown to Lower Lake, then continue north on Highway 53 to Highway 20. Turn right and drive east on Highway 20 for 5.5 miles. Just before the bridge over North Fork Cache Creek, a gravel road leaves the south side of the highway, leading to the trailhead parking lot in 0.2 mile. There is a new restroom facility and room for about 25 vehicles, including horse trailers and RVs.

DISTANCE: 8 miles to south end of Wilson Valley, 16 miles round trip.

GRADE: Moderate

BEST TIME: Spring, fall.

DOGS ALLOWED: On leash

INFO: Bureau of Land Management, Ukiah 707/468-4000

SUGGESTIONS: A pair of old tennies is very handy for fording Cache Creek at Baton Flat.

CAMPING: There are no developed campsites, but primitive camping is permitted starting ¼ mile beyond the trailhead. Campfires are not allowed during the fire season.

WARNINGS: The ford at Baton Flat is not safe at high water. Go to www.dreamflows.com for daily updates on California and Nevada rivers. An alternate site that also works is http://water.usgs.gov/waterwatch. Purify all water, preferably using springs and the smaller creeks.

TRAIL NOTES:

Pick up a map, sign the register and stride through the gate onto the level gravel path. You'll see western redbud, the pride of Yolo and Lake counties, which blooms during March and April. You may hear the familiar sounds of the cheerful meadowlark, distant lowing cattle, and the half alarm bell, half strangled yelp of wild turkey, or was that a hunter wringing its neck?

At ⅛ mile depart the gravel road onto a dirt road signed for hikers and equestrians. Butter and eggs are among the several species of tiny flowers. Cross a fifty-foot-wide seasonal wash and pick up a single track on the other side. Gray pines, manzanita, and oaks shelter Indian warrior, hound's tongue, shooting stars and clingy bedstraw in spring. Climb slightly, then parallel the big field to the north, in cultivation since the 1870s. On the other side of the highway are spectacular eroded cliffs that yield beautiful colors in the evening light, reminding one more of southern Utah than northern California.

Around ½ mile the trail begins to climb in earnest, soon crossing a seasonal creek. Chaparral species emerge like

Dramatic cliffs along Cache Creek

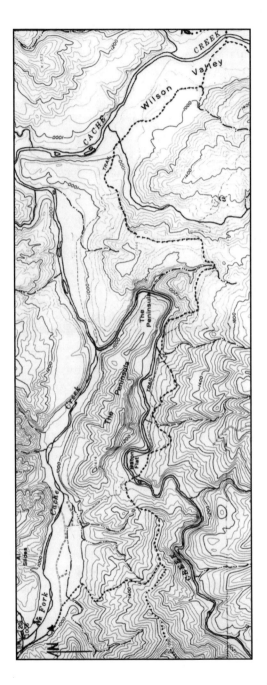

ceanothus and mountain mahogany as the trail switchbacks higher. Indian warrior and shooting star here seem to congregate under manzanita more than other shrubs or trees. The first views of Cache Creek Canyon appear at mile 1. At 1⅜ miles you top the ridge. The spine of this ridge holds many picturesque white oaks, a favorite destination for picnickers. The great brushy mass of the rather poetic sounding Brushy Sky High (3,196 feet), the highest peak in the Cache Creek Wilderness Area, rises across the main stem of Cache Creek.

Now drop gradually down the broad spine of the ridge looking for early spring wildflowers on this sunny slope. Start your main descent to Baton Flat around 1¾ miles. The trail mimics the sweeping curves of the river below as it switchbacks through a spring extravaganza of Indian warrior, truly the largest and finest around. Look for the incomparable Mariposa lily in late spring around mile 2. Another ½ mile of descent lands you on Baton Flat. The black walnuts planted in the 1880s by Great Britain emigre Billy Baton are found among the oaks on this side of the river. Be careful venturing off trail where numerous ground squirrel burrows await the unwary.

Do not attempt to cross Cache Creek in high water. In low conditions an old pair of tennies will save your hiking boots and socks from a soaking. You don't want to cross barefoot as the ford is rocky and in places slippery with moss.

Pick up a jeep trail briefly on the flat across the river, go about ⅛ mile then veer right at the trail sign. The jeep trail will dead end at the creek due to a landslide, very common here. Ascend a bit, then traverse oak woodlands. Just after mile 3 continue on the path straight across an intersecting double track. Make a short descent to the river flood plain and a small creek before 3½ miles. Be on the lookout for golden eagles which are fairly common throughout the year. At this point on my hike, I flushed out three of these raptors who flew down the creek.

Follow the river for a short stretch. The jeep trail continues on into private property while the trail climbs briefly to another terrace then traverses it for about ½ mile. You may see flickers and jays in this riparian corridor and even a pileated woodpecker. Descend to a junction near the river again where you have two choices. A double track that diagonals up the hill leads to a meadow where the rare and beautiful pink Adobe lily (Fritillaria pluriflora) blooms in March and April. The second choice, a bypass to the left, joins this same track beyond the meadow. At 4½ miles you encounter a nice overlook of a narrow gorge and a great view of the ridge called The Peninsula.

The double track becomes single again before a distinct rock outcrop, then joins a jeep trail at 4¾ miles. If you have a water filter, the little creek is a good early season source of water, the last one before Wilson Valley. Follow the jeep road left for 500 feet to another junction. You may continue on the jeep trail which is more direct, or on the trail to your left. The trail will lead you to a glade and another site for Adobe lilies. Before 5⅜ miles the trail joins the jeep track again and goes left, where ceanothus blooms in winter and early spring. Around 5⅝ miles a sign points left onto a wide path through a sea of chamise. Yerba buena takes advantage of the recent clearings by the trailside.

You have your first views into Wilson Valley, then an unmarked side path on the right leads 300 feet to a superb dry camp in a blue oak grove. This offers a good place to drop the pack and hike on unencumbered if you plan to camp here. Continue along the ridgetop, then before mile 6 you begin a steep descent. At one point only a thin, crumbly bank separates you from a badly eroded gully. Connect with a jeep trail and reach the transparently named Rocky Creek where huge gray pines grow. The ford should be an easy rock hop over clear water. If you approach Wilson Valley at first light when dappled early morning sun filters through the pines and oaks, the expansive grasslands and wildflowers and the peace and quiet of this secluded valley make it seem like you're entering an abandoned paradise.

A middle, higher ground beyond mile 7 separates the two enormous, previously cultivated fields of Wilson Valley. The valley oaks increase in size and grandeur in this middle ground. At 7½ miles the trail drops slightly and passes old fruit trees next to a creekbed on the west side, the site of the old homestead owned by James Brenard. Take the level trail through the lower grassy field until progress comes to an abrupt halt at Cache Creek. Return the same way, or if the creek is safe to cross, you can explore the Judge Davis Trail which starts at the southeast end of Wilson Valley.

JUDGE DAVIS TRAIL

DIRECTIONS: From Napa Valley, take Highway 29 north past Mount St. Helena and Middletown to Lower Lake, then continue north on Highway 53 for 7.5 miles to Highway 20. Turn right and drive east on Highway 20 for 14.6 miles to mile marker 46.07. Park in the large lot on the right (south) side of the highway beside the old wooden sheep corral. Do not take the more obvious fire road to its left but the trail on the right side.

DISTANCE 10¼ miles or more round trip

GRADE: Strenuous

BEST TIME: Fall, spring

ELEVATION GAIN: 1300 feet

SUGGESTIONS: Avoid this hike when the trail is wet. The adhering nature of the soil causes it to clump under boot heels as fast as it can be removed. Bring binoculars and telephoto camera lens for fantastic wildlife viewing opportunities. If you go in summer, treat it like a desert hike and take a minimum one gallon of water per person. A pair of old tennies is very handy for fording Cache Creek.

CAMPING: There are no developed campsites, but primitive camping is permitted starting ¼ mile beyond the trailhead. Campfires are not allowed during the fire season.

WARNINGS: Due to road work on Highway 20, use caution when driving into the steep parking lot entrance of 10% grade. The ford of Cache Creek is not safe at high water. Go to www. dreamflows.com for daily updates on California and Nevada rivers. An alternate site that also works is http://water.usgs.gov/waterwatch. Purify all water, preferably using springs and the smaller creeks.

TRAIL NOTES:

Parallel the highway briefly through blue oak woodland. As the vegetation gets scrubbier, toyon, redbud, cercocarpus and some gray pine will show. Before ¼ mile turn sharply left at a small streambed where star thistle has invaded. Cross the stream again and start climbing at the BLM horse trail marker. This trail was designed mainly for equestrian use so be forewarned — horses don't mind steep trails.

Walk through a pure stand of blue oak woodland around ⅜ mile. The blue oak has the greatest range of all the oaks in California; the hotter and drier the hillside the better. It is said an irrigation ditch cut too near the blue oak will gradually kill it. After a steep section at ½ mile, look behind you for a first view of Blue Ridge, named of course for the blue oak. Off the trail is a small, round swale that may have been a stock pond when sheep were grazed here.

Come out into open chamise country at another steep section, then surmount Cache Creek Ridge beyond ¾ mile. The views from here are sterling. Little Blue Ridge to the south helps contain Wilson Valley (still out of sight), the heart of the Cache Creek Management Area. To the west is a great snapshot of Clear Lake's dormant volcano, Mount Konocti. Descend briefly to the fire road and turn left at the junction.

At mile 1 is a signed trail fork. Cache Creek Ridge Trail

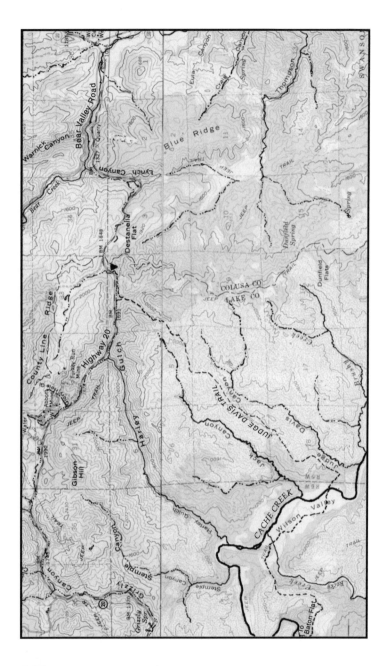

goes left, but you head downhill on the Judge Davis Trail. Here the simple nature of the trail becomes all too clear — it's a long, long way down the ridgeline. No way to get lost though. The fire road turns to double track passing through extensive grasslands. Entire mountainsides of uniform chamise surround you, perhaps punctuated by a single, mighty gray pine while in the creek beds, bright green pockets of cottonwood liven up the sepia-washed slopes that spread to the horizon.

The double track ends at a hilltop at 1½ miles after a brief climb, then dives down an absurdly steep slope, turning to wide trail. Beyond 2¼ miles pass one of several blue oak groves on the trail. By the size of the trunks, considering they grow more slowly than most oaks, I estimate the largest of these to be around 200 years old. From now on the sea of chamise will be pleasantly broken by a series of these groves. A first peek at Wilson Valley comes beyond 2⅝ miles. At three miles, round a scrubby hillside and look way down Cache Creek Canyon. The big landslide scar in the vicinity of Crack Canyon is from the 1906 earthquake that rocked San Francisco and dammed this canyon with a lake for five days (see Blue Ridge chapter).

Pass two more lovely oak groves perfect for resting, snacking, lunching or napping, the first at 3⅛ miles, the second at 3½ miles. You might see a covey of quail here or woodpeckers searching for insects, some of the more than 150 species of birds documented in the Cache Creek Management Area. To this point only the north end of Wilson Valley has been visible, but at 4 miles all of the two mile-long valley comes into view. At 4½ miles oak groves predominate. Stay left at an unmarked junction, then take switchbacks to the flood plain above Cache Creek at 5⅛ miles. If the water is high Wilson Valley is inaccessible. Never mind. Take a well deserved rest and look for river otters. On my visit I saw four of the playful critters, diving skillfully for crayfish and chowing them down with relish. In winter bald eagles are plentiful.

Return the same way. If the water is low and you shuttled a vehicle to the Redbud Trailhead, you can return via the Redbud Trail.

Wilson Valley seen from the Judge Davis Trail

ACKNOWLEDGMENTS

continued from page 6

Duane Smith of Solano Audubon, David Storck and Mike Sanford-Brown of the Petrified Forest, Tony Cerar, Helen Enos, Supervisors Mel Varrelman and Paul Batiste, Napa Planning Director John Yost, Kevin Williams, Barbara Stafford, Gina Urbani, Barbara Pahre, Ed Reynolds, Earl Balch and Dave Briggs.

Key sources for the second edition were Julie Burcell of BLM, Dan Tolson of UC Davis, Teri Geiger of Rockville Hills, Glenn Salva of Atlas Peak Vineyards, Dee Swanhuyser of Bay Area Ridge Trail Council, geologist turned winemaker John Livingston, and Sieg, George, Milo and Karl at the Vets' Home archives. Lastly, thanks to Andrew Fulks for his knowledge and passion for the wilds of the region.

For the third edition, Steve Ehret of Sonoma County Regional Parks provided invaluable help on the Hood Mountain chapter. Thanks to Ken Poerner, Land Steward, and Dave Warner, docent, at Lynch Canyon. Paul Aigner and Cathy Koehler at McLaughlin UC Reserve introduced me to Earle Swift who generously loaned me a copy of the Owen History manuscript. John Woodbury, General Manager of Napa County Open Space District, answered many questions on the Oat Hill Mine Trail situation. A special thanks again to Barbara Stafford who answered my many questions on the Napa River Trail. My hiking partners Kiya Cote, Carole Kunze, Lee Loban, Tanya Fisher, Vicki Greenbaum, and Isabelle St. Guily kept me company and offered suggestions. Sam Bledsoe provided information on Fiske Creek.

SUGGESTED READING

Calkins, Victoria, *The Wappo People*, Pileated Press, Santa Rosa, California, 1994.

Grieg, Jack R., *The Vessels of the Napa River*, Napa County Historical Society (from *Gleanings*), Napa, California, 1984.

Griffiths, Edith R., *Exploration For Oil in Berryessa Valley*, Napa County Historical Society (from *Gleanings*), Napa, 1970.

Lange, Dorothea and Pirkle Jones, *Death of a Valley*, Aperture, Inc., New York, 1960.

Lyman, W.W. Jr., *The Lyman Family*, Napa County Historical Society, (from *Gleanings*), Napa, 1980.

Manson, Michael W., *Landslide and Flood Potential Along Cache Creek*, adapted from *Landslide Hazards along Cache Creek between Clear Lake and Capay Valley, Lake, Colusa, and Yolo counties*, California Division of Mines and Geology Open-File Report 89-30, May, 1990.

Mattison, Elise, *California's Fossil Forest of Sonoma County*, from *California Geology*, September, 1990.

McKenzie, Robert E., *The Monticello Rodeo and Barbecue*, Napa County Historical Society (from *Gleanings*), Napa, 1975.

Neelands, Barbara, *Reason Tucker, The Quiet Pioneer*, Napa County Historical Society (from *Gleanings*), Napa, 1989.

Owen, Frank, *Early Days at Zem Zem*, first hand personal account, Napa County Historical Association

Stanton, Ken, *Mount St. Helena and Robert Louis Stevenson State Park, a history and guide*, Bonnie View Books, Saint Helena, California, 1997.

Stevenson, Robert Louis, *The Silverado Squatters*, Lewis Osborne, Ashland, Oregon, 1974,

Stewart, George Rippey Jr., *Stevenson in California, A Critical Study*, Master's Thesis, University of California, Berkeley, 1920.

Swift, Ida Owen, *History of the Owen Family*, hand written manuscript, 1935

Tortorolo, Mario J., *History of the City of Napa Water Supply*, Napa County Historical Society, (from *Gleanings*), Napa, 1978.

Verardo, Jennie and Denzil, *Dr. Edward Turner Bale and His Grist Mill*, Napa County Historical Society, (from *Gleanings*), Napa, 1979.

Walters and Larkey, *Yolo County, Land of Changing Patterns*, Windsor Press, Windsor, California, 1987.

Wichels, John, *There is the Yountville Camp Grounds, So What?*, Napa County Historical Society, Napa, 1982.

SUGGESTED WEB SITES

http://www.Yolohiker.org
Enthusiastic and detailed trail descriptions of but not limited to the Cache Creek Wilderness Area. Led hike program fall through spring.

http://www.BerryessaTrails.org
Information on trails, boating, and updates on the rapidly changing recreation scene at Lake Berryessa

http://nrs.ucdavis.edu/stebbins
Entertaining and scholarly natural history information of Stebbins Cold Canyon Reserve

INDEX

Every trail mentioned in the text is indexed

ABOUT THE AUTHOR

Ken's life long participation in the outdoors includes hiking, backpacking, mountaineering and whitewater boating in the United States, Canada, Mexico, Costa Rica and Europe. He lives in the Napa Valley and has worked in the wine grape industry for twenty-five years. He has published two other books, *Mount St. Helena and Robert Louis Stevenson State Park, a history and guide* (1993) and co-authored *Napa Valley Picnic* with Jack Burton (2001).

Photograph by Kiya Cote

ABOUT BORED FEET

We began Bored Feet in 1986 to publish *The Hiker's hip pocket Guide to the Mendocino Coast*. We've grown our company by providing the most accurate guidebooks for California, including the award-winning two-volume series, *Hiking the California Coastal Trail*. Thank you for supporting quality independent publishing with your purchase, helping us to bring you more information about gorgeous and fascinating California. We love to hear your feedback about this or any of our other products.

Updates for several of our books are available at our website, **www.boredfeet.com**, where you can easily order any or all of our great books and maps. You can also get updates or a catalog by sending us your name and address, specifying your areas of interest.

We offer quick (standard shipping) and lightning fast (rush) order for the more than 150 books and 100 maps we carry about California and the West. **To order items, go to www.boredfeet.com, or send name, address, check or money order, or call one of the phone numbers listed below for Visa/Mastercard purchases. Please add $3 shipping for orders under $30, $5 over $30 ($5/7 for rush).**

Titles below represent just a portion of our complete catalog.

Hiker's hip pocket Guide to the Mendocino Coast, 3rd ed.,Lorentzen	$15.00
Hiker's hip pocket Guide to Sonoma County, 3rd edition,Lorentzen	16.00
Hiker's hip pocket Guide to the Humboldt Coast, 2nd ed.,Lorentzen	15.00
Hiker's hip pocket Guide to the Mendocino Highlands, 2nd ed.,"	17.00
Hiking the CA Coastal Trail, Vol. One: Oregon to Monterey, 2nd ed.,"	19.50
Hiking the California Coastal Trail, Vol. Two: Monterey to Mexico	19.00
Hiking the California Coastal Trail Gift Set: Volumes 1 & 2	37.00
Geologic Trips: San Francisco & the Bay Area, Konigsmark	13.95
Geologic Trips: Sierra Nevada, Konigsmark	17.50
Great Day Hikes in & around Napa Valley, 3rd edition, Stanton	16.00
Sonoma Picnic: CA Wine Country Guide, Burton	9.95
Napa Valley Picnic: CA Wine Country Guide, Burton & Stanton	9.95
Mendocino Coast Glove Box Guide, 3rd edition, Lorentzen	17.50
Trails & Tales of Yosemite & the Central Sierra, Giacomazzi	17.50
Exploring Eastern Sierra Canyons: Sonora Pass to Pine Creek,"	15.50
Day Trips with a Splash: Swimming Holes of California, Doll	18.95

For shipping to a California address, please add 7.25% sales tax.

PRICES SUBJECT TO CHANGE WITHOUT NOTICE.
BORED FEET PRESS
www.boredfeet.com
P.O. Box 1832
Mendocino, CA 95460
888-336-6199 • 707-964-6629